Good si

D1241310

ROAD TRIP EATS

ROAD TRIP EATS

101 Places Across *Ya Gotta Eat Here*

KENTUCKY *with Recipes!*

Gary P. West

Acclaim Press
MORLEY, MISSOURI

Acclaim Press
— *Your Next Great Book* —
P.O. Box 238
Morley, MO 63767
(573) 472-9800
www.acclaimpress.com

Book Designer: Devon Burroughs
Cover Design: M. Frene Melton

Cover photos: *A 1962 Corvette, owned by Rik and Sandy Hawkins, in front of an Andy Griffith-inspired replica garage, sits adjacent to the Hawkin's home in Hardin County just outside of Elizabethtown. Rik is looking over a Kentucky map with author Gary P. West and wife, Deborah. Photographs courstesy of David Toczko.*

Library of Congress Control Number: 2015934564
ISBN:13: 978-1-938905-98-8
ISBN-10: 1-938905-98-9

First Printing: 2015
Printed in the United States of America
10 9 8 7 6 5 4 3 2 1

This publication was produced using available information.
The Publisher regrets it cannot assume responsibility for errors or omissions.

Contents

Preface.. 6

Introduction 8

Western Region.....................................12

Central Region 56

South Central Region 122

Northern Region 160

Eastern Region 186

Recipes 220

About the Author 254

Index.. 258

Restaurant Index................................ 263

Recipe Index 266

Preface

Agourmet dining guide? Hardly. You won't find what are referred to as "fine dining" restaurants in this book. In all of them, however, you will find good food reasonably priced.

Candlelight dinners, eating gourmet foods, is not what *Road Trip Eats* is all about, but simple food is.

None of the restaurants in this book have paid for their inclusion. The only way an eatery made the "101 list" was to be recommended by someone who lives in the area, often people in the tourism and hospitality business, or by my personal experience.

Deborah and I spent more than a year doing the research required … experiencing the cuisine that is unique to Kentucky bite by bite. We literally traveled the state from one end to the other, east to west, and north to south. The visits were memorable, for not only the food we ate, but the people we met.

When it comes to Kentucky's scenery, if you're new to the state, you are in for a treat. Those of you who have been around for a while may have forgotten how really beautiful this state is.

From the flatlands in the west, to the rolling hills in the central, to the breathtaking mountains in the east, travelers can easily be distracted and miss certain turns and even road signs. That's part of the experience.

Winding roads, grained-filled silos with nearby grazing cattle, country churches, neatly trimmed fence rows and lots of farm houses whose occupants I knew were the heartbeat of not only Kentucky, but America, made our periodic excursions worthwhile.

Beauty is indeed in the eye of the beholder. It can be a memorable moment when you see a glistening lake that can put you in a trance with the sun sparkling on the dancing ripples.

It's amazing how many people, when planning a trip, make where to eat a part of it. One of the most often asked questions is, "Where are we going to eat?" *Road Trip Eats* takes the guesswork out of it.

The book is a bit more than a guide to good places to eat. It's a must-keep history that documents our Kentucky heritage as it relates to down home comfort food, many of which are very casual, while others are in a more upscale atmosphere.

It has been said that the five southern food groups are sugar, salt, butter, cream and grease. And it can also be said that most of Kentucky's working class cooks and certified chefs use most or all of these items when turning out good eats.

Road Trip Eats goes even further, even presenting popular recipes from several of the restaurants. May I suggest that you document your visit to these eateries by dating the time of your visit and even what you ate. What a neat gift to pass on to your children or grandchildren!

Introduction

One doesn't have to look far to find good places to eat across Kentucky. There are literally thousands, and I'm not talking about "fast food", either.

Road Trip Eats makes your search much, much easier, and the fact that this book focuses on mostly mom and pop places, many of which are located in the far reaches on the back roads of Kentucky, travelers will find something to their liking in the bigger cities, too.

In these pages the state has been divided into five geographical regions to make it more user friendly.

For inclusion, a restaurant could not be a chain, and must have had their doors open for at least five years. There are a few exceptions to the latter. My goal is to identify restaurants that perhaps you may not visit unless you have this book. You can be sure, however, that every eatery here is known to their locals and now have been exposed to the outsiders.

There are many outstanding chains and independents in our state, and their omission is not a reflection of their quality. This is only a guide to restaurants that my wife Deborah and I have personally visited, much like what hospitality guru Duncan Hines, a Kentuckian from Bowling Green, first did in the 1930's and into the 1950's. He did it across America, while I have concentrated on Kentucky.

As people's travel habits began to change in the '60s with the construction of interstates and increased popularity of air travel, guidebooks lost their zest. Public travel had become all about getting there, with little interest in between.

But now that has changed. There *is* a large segment of travelers who have reverted back to yesteryear, no longer in such a hurry to get to where they are going as they once were.

Road Trip Eats encourages people to not only enjoy the beautiful scenery in Kentucky, but to meet some friendly people and taste the mighty fine food they serve.

If you are traveling a long distance to eat in one of the listed restaurants, it is suggested you may want to call ahead to verify hours of operation. Remember time zone changes.

It is further suggested that you check to make sure these restaurants are open, particularly if you are making the trip just for the dining. Because some of these restaurants are indeed "backroads" establishments, they sometime alter their hours of operation. Some even shut down for seasonal breaks. This is noted on several listings.

Visitors unfamiliar with Kentucky law should be aware that several county jurisdictions throughout the state do not permit the sale of alcohol.

At press time, menu items were confirmed. These, too, change. And any directions given here are for reference only. You might want to stop and ask the locals for more specifics, as a GPS isn't always accurate on the backroads. This can be part of the enjoyment, and hopefully add to your roadtrip experience.

Give yourself a challenge. Plan a road trip now. So get up, get out and get going!

ROAD TRIP EATS

101 Places Across *Ya Gotta Eat Here*

Places Across

KENTUCKY

with Recipes!

Blue & White Grill	Hazel, KY
Catfish Kitchen	Draffenville, KY
Commonwealth Kitchen & Bar	Henderson, KY
The Crowded House	Madisonville, KY
Dairy Freeze	Island, KY
DaVinci's Little Italian Restaurant	Hopkinsville, KY
Dinner Bell	Benton, KY
Dixie Pan Restaurant	Nortonville, KY
Doe's Eat Place	Paducah, KY
Gold Rush Café	Paducah, KY
KayLee's Farmhouse Restaurant	Aurora, KY
Knoth's BarBQue	Lake City, KY
Lake Barkley, Kenlake, Kentucky Dam Village	Cadiz, Hardin, Gilbertsville, KY
Lite Side Café & Bakery	Grand Rivers, KY
Miller House	Owensboro, KY
Mugsy's Hideout	Murray, KY
Parcell's Deli & Grill	Benton, KY
Reva's Place	Cadiz, KY
Rookies Food & Spirits	Henderson, KY
Short's Family Restaurant	Graham, KY
Wild Mountain Bakery & Café	Murray, KY

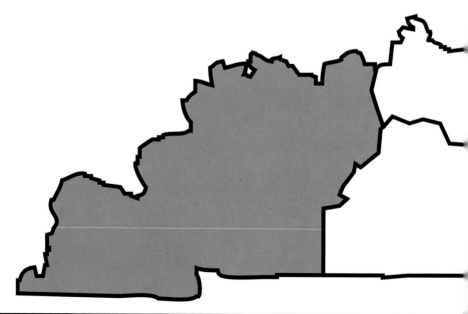

WESTERN REGION

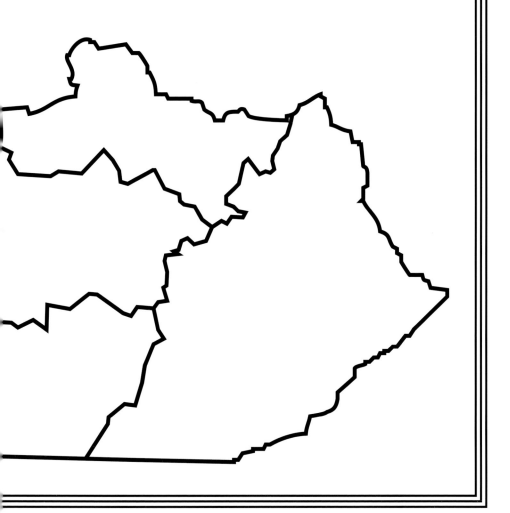

Blue & White Grill

Hazel is a small village known for its antiques that sits close to the Kentucky-Tennessee state line, about eight miles from Murray. When Scooter Paschall and his wife Barb opened a restaurant a few years ago, it was the name of it that might have been a surprise to some of their nearby customers.

The Blue and White Grill was a natural.

"I love the Wildcats," Scooter says. "And yes, quite a bit of our business comes from Tennessee folks."

It just goes to show that good food can overcome a lot of differences, and in spite of the blue and white décor in the 70-seat restaurant, a truce is called when it comes time to eat.

Blue and White is a seven day restaurant that begins with breakfast and all of the classics, including pork chops, pork tenderloin, country ham, pancakes, French toast, and hashbrowns. Then there are the omelets, biscuit sandwiches, grits and biscuit and gravy.

Every day at lunchtime, a different assortment of meats, fish and vegetables are plated.

"We serve our plate lunches from 11 a.m. til closing time," says Barb.

The evening meal also offers several sandwich options, as well as appetizers, chicken Provolone, pork chops, ribeyes, catfish, and grilled shrimp.

"Our fried chicken is very popular," Scooter adds. "We hand batter it."

Barb makes the pies daily, and they serve it by the slice or whole.

"We sell a lot of pies here," she says. "We have chocolate, coconut, lemon ice box, pecan and even a sugar free apple."

A children's menu is available for breakfast and dinner.

Address:
318 Main Street
Hours:
Monday-Saturday, 6 a.m. – 8 p.m.
Sunday, 6 a.m. – 2 p.m.
Phone:
270-492-8195
Price Range: $$
Area Attractions:
Antiques, Murray State University

Catfish Kitchen

DRAFFENVILLE, KENTUCKY

When Wes and Judy Davis decided, in 1989, to make a career change, they probably had no idea that the restaurant they were opening would become one of the most popular ones in western Kentucky.

Wes had been in the business of running grocery stores and was well versed in food products, so when he took over a property that already had a pair of scenic ponds, Catfish Kitchen was a natural.

This restaurant opens at 4 p.m., and soon after it is full. The dining room overlooks the pond water features that have wooden decks where visitors stroll to before or after eating.

"We serve only U.S. farm raised fish," Wes offers. "It's a little more expensive, but it's well worth it."

As you sit down in the Catfish Kitchen, you are quickly served a bowl of white beans, slaw and some of the best hushpuppies you'll ever eat.

'We cook those beans three to four hours and hand roll each of our hushpuppies," adds Wes.

The offerings here include much more than catfish. Fried chicken strips, clam and shrimp dinners, and then there are the baked fish and baked chicken breast dinners. They prefer you call ahead on these, as they take longer to prepare.

Plentiful, too, are what the Catfish Kitchen calls their "munchies": breaded cheese-stuffed jalapenos, fried dills, onion rings, mozzarella cheese sticks, and semi-spicy green tomato relish.

Desserts include blackberry, peach and cherry cobblers, sugar cream pie, and chocolate sundaes.

Wes and Judy are quick to point out the success of their business has been loyal employees, one of which has been Gloria Mathis, who has been with them since they opened.

Catfish Kitchen closes the month of December.

DINERS INFORMATION

Address:
Hwy. 641 (Draffenville, 4 miles south of Kentucky Dam)
136 Teal Run Circle
Hours:
Wednesday-Saturday, 4 p.m. — 9 p.m.
Sunday, 11 a.m. — 9 p.m.
Closed Monday and Tuesday
Phone:
270-362-7306
Price Range: $$
Area Attractions:
Kentucky Lake, fishing, shopping

Commonwealth Kitchen & Bar

HENDERSON, KENTUCKY

When the owners of Commonwealth Kitchen & Bar, known to the locals as CKB, opened their "it's not quite a bar and not quite a restaurant," in Henderson, their goal was to do something different. And they have.

Owners Mark Logan and Jayson Munoz have perhaps created one of the most unique restaurants in the area, and that includes nearby Evansville, Indiana.

CKB is small, only seating 64, with a few seats at the bar, but the venue packs a wallop with both its industrial look and a not-so-run-of-the mill menu.

"We were inspired to create foods people around here would like and not have to go somewhere else to eat," says Munoz. "Why don't we have this in Henderson? Now we do."

From the exposed brick walls, to the metal chairs, mixed in with huge tin accent pieces, the bar area lays claim to the biggest bourbon collection in town.

But now, on to that menu.

Flavored by herbs and spices grown on their roof-top garden, steaks, seafood, lamb meatballs, and those oh so good pig wings are offered. The pig wings are served as mini pork shanks tossed in a special sauce. Salmon, shrimp and scallops are popular, as is Philly cheesesteak egg rolls.

"Believe it or not, our bestselling item is the Brussels Sprouts," adds Munoz. "We prepare it like nobody else."

If you don't have room for the dessert, at least take their signature dessert home with you. It's the raspberry cheesecake egg roll, with raspberry preserves surrounded by cheesecake filling wrapped in a light crust.

DINERS INFORMATION

Address:
108 2nd Street
Hours:
Monday-Wednesday, 11 a.m. – 9 p.m.
Thursday-Saturday, 11 a.m. – 10 p.m.
Closed Sunday
Phone:
270-212-2133
Price Range: $$
Area Attractions:
W.C. Handy Music Festival, John James Audubon State Park

The Crowded House

MADISONVILLE, KENTUCKY

The small sign hanging high above the door of The Crowded House in downtown Madisonville is not indicative of what you'll find inside. This is one fine restaurant that is rapidly making itself known as a destination place throughout several surrounding counties.

The menu is packed with appetizers that include a giant pretzel served in a 12" pizza box, jumbo shrimp cocktail, calamari, and lettuce wraps, and the beef and pork dishes, seafood and chicken, soups, salads, and a selection of burgers do, indeed, keep this restaurant crowded.

The boneless grilled pork ribeye will rival pork chops anywhere in western Kentucky. On the seafood side, the grilled salmon and the hand breaded gulf fried oysters will make you think the ocean is right outside the door.

Owners Cliff Nance and Jessie Garrett have recycled this old building to give it a slight industrial look with the corrugated tin and exposed brick walls. Early on they opened their doors as a muffin-sandwich shop with 64 seats. But now it has blossomed into one of the most talked about restaurants in the area, with 165 seats that include some of the largest, most

comfortable booths you'll ever sit in.

From the main dining room, customers can stroll into the connecting Green Dragon Tavern that takes its name from an old Boston tavern that lays claim to being in on the early planning of the American Revolution.

Chef Christina Cartwright has managed to bring her cooking skills and enthusiasm to the forefront in keeping in step with what Nance and Garrett are doing out front.

The Crowded House, whose name came from a church in the United Kingdom, can hold its own with restaurants in much bigger cities.

DINERS INFORMATION

Address:
26 West Center Street
Hours:
Tuesday-Saturday, 10:30 a.m. – 10 p.m.
Friday-Saturday, Tavern is open til 11 p.m.
Phone:
270-825-1178
Price Range: $$
Area Attractions:
Gov. Ruby Laffoon Log Cabin

Dairy Freeze

ISLAND, KENTUCKY

When Owsley Taylor opened up his Dairy Freeze in the very small community of Island, in McLean County, back in 1956, it would be a safe bet that he would never have thought that his little walk-up eatery would one day sell over 800 Island burgers every day, six days a week. The number is a little less than three times the town's population of 350.

Today, Henry Taylor, wife Lydia and their sons Tim and Don have a year-round business that is one of the most popular in a four county area.

"My wife had worked hard to build the business," says Henry, who started working for his dad at the age of 12." So we decided to buy it from my mom in 1979."

The Taylor's draw big crowds, and their 15 employees in the small block building with the big ice cream cone hanging out front, is easy to spot for those who are new to the area. Behind the blue-roofed Dairy Freeze is a large paved parking lot with several big picnic tables under a covered top to weather-proof the eating experience.

Henry Taylor is proud that in all of the 58 years, his restaurant has never served up a frozen burger. "We keep em' fresh, and only cook em' when they're ordered," he says.

This is much more than a burger, chili dog and shake place. The pork tenderloin is a big seller, too. An assortment of salads and breakfast sandwiches further show the range of what the Taylor family offers.

This is one little walk-up worth finding.

Address:
Hwy. 431
Open:
Monday-Saturday, 8 a.m. – 10:30 p.m.
Closed Sunday
Phone:
270-486-3213
Price Range: $
Area Attractions:
Coal fields

DaVinci's Little Italian Restaurant

There are some restaurants when you walk in, you just know they are the real deal. And that's exactly what DaVinci's Little Italian Restaurant is … the real deal.

It's what the sign out front says it is, a little Italian restaurant, but does it ever pack a big wallop with the food it serves.

"Our recipes have been passed down for generations after generations in northern Italy," says chef-owner Pavel Skorpil, who opened his Hopkinsville restaurant in 2009.

Chef Pavel came to the United States in 1999, and got his foot in the door of a Florida restaurant by washing dishes. He hasn't looked back since, working in Atlanta before moving to Kentucky and opening his restaurant at the insistence of his wife, Alexandra.

Everything served here is a masterpiece; from the house made Focaccia bread with the tasty garlic dipping oil, to the fettuccine alfredo, to the fried calamari, to the portabella mushroom ravioli, to the spaghetti and meatballs.

DaVinci's was a 2014 Trip Advisor Certificate of Excellence. "We were the only one in Kentucky," Chef Skorpil said.

With everything that's good, the real award winner may be the house made lasagna. It very well may be the best you've ever eaten.

Just talking to Pavel, one quickly hears and sees his passion and pride in what he serves. He takes no shortcuts with his food.

The restaurant seats about 60 inside that includes a small bar, and the patio can accommodate 18 more.

DINERS INFORMATION

Address:
304 North Drive
Hours:
Monday, 11 a.m. – 2 p.m. (Lunch); 4:30 – 8 p.m. (Dinner)
Friday, 11 a.m. – 2 p.m. (Lunch); 4 p.m. – 9 p.m. (Dinner)
Saturday, 12 a.m. – 2 p.m (Lunch); 4 p.m. – 9 p.m. (Dinner)
Closed Sunday
Phone:
270-874-2853
Price Range: $$
Area Attractions:
Ft. Campbell, Trail of Tears Park

Dinner Bell

BENTON, KENTUCKY

I t's all about family style cooking and eating at this Marshall County restaurant. Its selections are more like a smorgasbord with a "help yourself" style and an impressive salad bar.

Martha Hooper has been running things here since about 1980, and then recently grandson Harry Holliday has taken over the kitchen chores and the restaurant hasn't missed a beat.

This Thursday-Friday-Saturday-Sunday restaurant is a seasonal eatery only. But when they open their doors they are packed.

The presentation of the food here is unlike just about any place else you'll eat. Served in big kettles on turn-of-the century stoves in the rear of the restaurant, customers line up and serve themselves. Each day has its own specials. Thursday is referred to as Cook's Choice, Friday is country fried steak and gravy, Saturday, pork chops and gravy, and Sunday, turkey and dressing. As you can guess, there are plenty of vegetables to round out a great meal, country style.

But wait … there's more!

Fried chicken and catfish and the salad bar are served every day.

Large picnic tables serve as the restaurant's tables, and it all adds to the dining experience at the Dinner Bell.

This is a seasonal restaurant.

DINERS INFORMATION

Address:
13444 U.S. 68E (One mile East of Jonathon Creek Bridge)
Hours:
Thursday-Saturday, 4 p.m. — 8 p.m.
Sunday, 11:30 a.m. — 7:30 p.m.
Open first weekend in March, closed last weekend in October.
Phone:
270-354-6521
Price Range: $$
Area Attractions:
Lakes, fishing, shopping

Dixie Pan Restaurant

NORTONVILLE, KENTUCKY

There's been a restaurant on this property since about 1958, when the old Dixie Line Highway passed near a Pan Am service station that stood nearby.

Since 1990, the Dixie Pan has been owned and operated by Ruth Ann and Jerry Prowse, and now it is considered one of the most popular eateries in the area.

Breakfast is served six days a week beginning at 6 a.m. til 11 a.m.

The Dixie Pan is one of those restaurants that if they don't have it, you probably don't need it. They feature a special each day of the week that ranges from turkey and dressing, to meatloaf, roast beef, liver & onions, barbeque, ham, and yes, even stuffed green peppers. And then there are the dishes that go with them: whipped potatoes, green beans, corn, baked apples, white beans, cabbage, pinto beans and coleslaw.

If for some reason you can't find something to your liking with those choices, the Dixie Pan serves up dinners of fried chicken, country ham, chuck wagon steak, pork tenderloin, smoked pork chops, and shrimp,

chili, breaded mushrooms, baked potatoes, onion rings and fries.

Want more? How about a sandwich selection of almost 20 to choose from? You've got it at the Dixie Pan.

"We're proud of everything we serve," Ruth Ann says. "Our pies are homemade and baked daily."

Coconut, chocolate, chess, pecan, cherry and apple are all of the choices you have ... so very sorry if there's not something here to your liking.

Address:
Hwy. 41A & 62
Hours:
Monday-Tuesday, Thursday-Sunday, 6 a.m. – 9 p.m.
Closed Wednesday
Phone:
270-676-3106
Price Range: $
Area Attractions:
Ruby Lafoon's Log Cabin

Doe's Eat Place

PADUCAH, KENTUCKY

There's never a bad time to visit Paducah. For such a small city (27,000 population) there is so much to do. And one of those things is to eat.

The beautiful downtown riverfront features a restaurant right in the middle of it all with a unique name … Doe's Eat Place, at the corner of Broadway and Market.

Paul Signa, the owner and operator, has created a casual atmosphere with some not so casual food. Doe's Eat Place is far from fancy. By that it means no tablecloths or fluffy napkins. It's common for visitors in Paducah for two or three days to eat there twice in one day.

Catfish, chili, and tamales are a specialty, but it's Paul's variety of inch-thick steaks that Doe's Eat Place has become known for.

Paul's family history in the restaurant business dates back to 1941 in Greenville, Mississippi, and believe it or not, it was those tamales that sort of kicked it all off back then.

"They're a tradition with us even here in Paducah," Paul said. "It might be a Mexican dish, but we do it with a Southern touch. We serve them by themselves or with our homemade chili."

Catfish, shrimp, lobster tail, Mahi Mahi, boneless chicken breast, and spaghetti with gigantic meatballs are entrée listings.

Make no mistake, however, Doe's is all about their steaks. And they are big-time, from the filet mignon, ribeye, T-bone, porterhouse and sirloin. All of them are hand cut in the restaurant, and customers can order the T-bone and porterhouse all the way up to 3 lbs.

The desserts are something you might just want to make a special visit to Doe's to eat. A warm chocolate cobbler with a couple of scoops of vanilla bean ice cream, then drizzled with a combination of caramel and chocolate, is a winner. But then, too, is the gourmet turtle cheesecake and carrot cake, a four layer production with cream cheese topping squeezed between each layer.

Doe's also offers spaghetti and chicken strips for children.

DINERS INFORMATION

Address:
136 Broadway
Hours:
Monday-Thursday, 10 a.m. — 9 p.m.
Friday, 10 a.m. — 10 p.m.
Saturday, 11 a.m. — 10 p.m.
Sunday, 11 a.m. — 9 p.m.
Phone:
270-443-9006
Price Range: $$$
Area Attractions:
Floodwall murals, National Quilt Museum, carriage rides, historic art district

Gold Rush Café

Ken White and wife, Anita, decided to purchase the Gold Rush Café in 2011. Located in downtown Paducah when they bought it, the restaurant was doing okay.

"We wanted to make it even better … more fun to eat here … get people talking about us," Ken said. "So we changed every recipe and began offering unique breakfasts."

White trained at the Orlando Culinary Academy, interned at Disney World's Epcot, and cooked in the Germany Pavilion in the World Showcase. That's where he met his wife.

After being away from Paducah for several years, he returned and was a part of the dining scene at several Paducah local restaurants before deciding to give the Gold Rush a go.

And a go it is. Using his creative kitchen skills, he is turning out breakfast and lunch selections not found anywhere else in town.

"We're the only place around serving Scotch eggs," he says. "And we even have input from our customers to help us decide on what our Saturday waffle special will be, by posting our "Waffle-Off on facebook. They put up suggestions and the one with the most "likes" wins."

The menu offers several

of the old standbys you'd expect on any breakfast and lunch menu, but it's those out-of-the norm creations that customers leave the Gold Rush talking about.

Here's some examples: carrot cake waffles, chocolate chip cookie dough waffles, peach cobbler waffles, gingerbread bacon, apple waffles and chocolate chess pie waffles.

"We make about 95% of our menu from scratch, including our biscuits, both the yeast and angel biscuits, hashbrowns, rolls and pancake batter," Ken points out.

Breakfast is an all-day thing with lots of omelets, with the selections often changing in the 50 seat restaurant.

Gold Rush is a three meal a day eatery, with specials being created as quickly as Ken White can think 'em up.

Address:
400 Broadway
Hours:
Tuesday-Saturday, 7 a.m. – 9 p.m.
Sunday, 9 a.m. – 2 p.m.
Closed Monday
Phone:
270-443-4422
Price Range: $
Area Attractions:
National Quilt Museum, Flood Wall Murals, Antiques, Lower Town Art District, Ohio River

KayLee's Farmhouse Restaurant

AURORA, KENTUCKY

Along about 1994 two sisters got together to open a restaurant in Aurora; one was named Kay and the other Lee. Now, we know where the restaurant's name came from. And then in 2005, Mary Lou Flynn bought the restaurant and has continued to churn out eats that attract visitors, but the locals as well. When the locals eat here, you know it's good.

There's nothing high-hat about KayLee's. It's a concrete block building with a concrete floor, but there's not a thing wrong with that. Neither is anything wrong with the food.

Breakfast begins at 6 a.m., seven days a week.

"We're kind of seasonal here," Mary Lou says. "We close the Sunday before Thanksgiving and open again the first week of March. And then in the spring we open at 5 a.m. to take care of all those early morning fishermen."

Saturday and Sunday's KayLee's serves a breakfast buffet that has 15 items. There are all kinds of egg combos that include bacon, sausage, and country ham and on and on, but there's one item that has everyone talking: KayLee's Special Potatoes. It is hash browns with green peppers, onion, tomatoes, ham, cheese, and mushrooms. The full order is so big that a half-order is offered. If someone doesn't like scrambled eggs they'll even fry, boil or poach your eggs on request.

Plate lunch specials are served all seven days, each featuring a different meat.

"Our meatloaf is really popular on Friday," says MaryLou. "And our burgers are the best. We hand pat them out fresh."

KayLee's is one of those places that doesn't have the big flashy sign out front. Just remember, you're there for the food. And, it speaks for itself.

Address:
15649 U.S. Hwy. 68E
Hours:
7 days a week, 6 a.m. – 2 p.m.
(Checks and cash accepted; no credit or debit cards)
Phone:
270-354-9875
Price Range: $
Area Attractions:
Lakes, fishing, Hitching Post & Old Country Store, Moonshine Museum

Knoth's BarBQue

LAKE CITY, KENTUCKY

This is a real, no-kiddin' barbeque place. First opened in 1965 by Leonard and Frances Knoth, son Hugh and his wife have carried on the tradition in fine fashion.

With five concrete block fire pits in a separate smoke house, Hugh can handle as many as 100 pork shoulders at one time. "We actually sold 150 of them in one day," he says.

At Knoth's it's all about simplicity. "We keep it simple here," Hugh adds. No beans, no potato salad. We do slaw and do it good. That's why we've been around so long."

Pork is the big seller here, but the beef brisket also goes good. "When we sell out, we close. I hang a sign in the window that says 'Sold out of Meat'," Hugh says.

"I grew up in the business," says Hugh. "We had a place in Lyon County, but it burned in 1992 and we moved here to Livingston County. The pit caught fire and burned our restaurant down. That's why I now have my pit in a separate building."

Knoth's, over the years, has been mentioned on the Johnny Carson and Jay Leno shows.

"Leno was making fun about a free glass of water we offered with each meal," Hugh laughed.

Knoth's also offers hot dogs, burgers, grilled cheese, fries and milk shakes.

"We keep our dessert simple, too," he adds. "Soft served ice cream."

The 100-seat restaurant is located next to Barkley Dam, not far from Grand Rivers and they, like many of the lake-area restaurants, are somewhat seasonal.

They open in mid-March and close after the first Saturday in November ... and they accept cash and checks only (no credit cards).

Address:
728 U.S. Hwy. 62
Hours:
Monday-Thursday, 11 a.m. — 7 p.m.
Friday-Saturday, 11 a.m. — 8 p.m.
Closed Sunday
Phone:
270-362-8580
Price Range: $
Area Attractions:
Lakes, fishing, boating, hunting

Lake Barkley, Kenlake, Kentucky Dam Village

CADIZ, HARDIN, GILBERTSVILLE, KENTUCKY

You've got to travel far and wide to find state parks like you'll find in Kentucky, so don't waste your time. In western Kentucky you'll find three State Parks, all within an easy hour drive of each other, that not only offer comfortable lodging, major marina access, challenging golf, but, best of all, good ole traditional southern comfort food to enjoy.

Lake Barkley and its Window on the Water dining room, Kenlake and Aurora Landing Restaurant, and what some might consider the crown jewel of Kentucky State Parks, Kentucky Dam Village and its Harbor Light dining room, all serve up delightful three-squares a day year-round.

The three resort parks sit in somewhat of a triangle, with a common attachment to Kentucky Lake and Lake Barkley.

A tradition at all three parks is the Kentucky Hot Brown with baked country ham, roasted turkey, smothered in a cheese sauce, topped with tomato, bacon and cheddar cheese and then baked to a golden brown. An assortment of sandwiches is offered as well.

Of course, breakfast is big. Omelets, pancakes, and biscuits and gravy are good, but the best part may be the fantastic views of the lake while dining.

At Harbor Lights Restaurant at Kentucky Dam Village, the menu is stepped up a bit. The dining room is easily accessible by boaters, who can tie-off and then walk up, and dine on ribeyes,

Black Angus top sirloins, chicken Amaretto, and all-you-can-eat farm raised catfish.

The parks are known for their Kentucky Proud participation that includes, Harper country hams, Purnell's sausage, John Conti coffee, and awesome Holiday buffets.

DINERS INFORMATION

Address/Phone:
Lake Barkley Resort Park
  3500 State Park Road, Cadiz, KY
  270-924-1131
Kenlake Resort Park
  542 Kenlake Road, Hardin, KY
  270-474-2211
Kentucky Dam Village Resort Park
  166 Upper Village, Hwy. 641, Gilbertsville, KY
  270-362-4271

Hours:
Breakfast, 7:00 a.m. – 10:00 a.m.
Lunch, 11:00 a.m. – 3:00 p.m.
Dinner, 4:00 p.m. – 9:00 p.m.

Price Range: $$

Area Attractions:
Marinas, Hiking, Lodging, Camping, Fishing, Swimming, Riding Stables

Lite Side Café & Bakery

GRAND RIVERS, KENTUCKY

Lite and bakery are two words that usually don't go together. But in beautiful Grand Rivers, Bob and Irene Bryan have made it work at their Lite Side Café and Bakery.

Being joined at the hips to two of Kentucky's most prominent lakes, Kentucky and Barkley, visitors are rarely without a view of the water.

Lite Side probably sits a bit under the food radar of western Kentucky, but once customers stop by, they are hooked much like many of the fish in the nearby lakes.

Speaking of hooks, at Lite Side the bakery might be what gets people in the door. The cookies, muffins, rolls and donuts are good, but so, too, are Brunswick stew, and what they call the Gobbler sandwich. Described as Thanksgiving on a bun, the sandwich consists of roast turkey on a home-made bun with lettuce, Swiss cheese, cream cheese, and cranberry sauce.

An assortment of unusual sandwiches, all assembled between fresh baked buns, gives customers something different.

"We're known for our bison burgers," Irene says. "It's ground buffalo meat that we perfectly grill."

The Black Bean Burger might look like a burger, but it's not a burger at all. It is black beans compressed with corn into a burger form, and served with salsa, lettuce and tomato on the side.

For those who want breakfast, Lite Side can take care of that, too.

Casseroles, breakfast quesadilla, sausage and ham sandwiches, croissant, eggs Benedict, sausage or ham, French toast, pancakes, and Belgian waffles are among the choices.

Lite Side Café and Bakery is open four days a week - Thursday, Friday, Saturday and Sunday, year-round.

DINERS INFORMATION

Address:
2063 Dover Road
Hours:
Thursday-Sunday, 8 a.m. – 2 p.m.
Phone:
270-362-4586
Price Range: $$
Area Attractions:
Kentucky Lake, Lake Barkley, Green Turtle Bay, Lighthouse Landing Marina

Miller House

The Miller House wouldn't be out of place in any city in America.

For three years, Jenne and Larry Kirk labored to restore one of Owensboro's historic old homes and convert it into a restaurant. And what a restaurant they opened in 2009. They are proof that this city has more than bar-b-que.

Known far and wide, The Miller House has become a destination restaurant, thanks in part to daughter Kasey Kirk-Dillow, who works along husband Jason to use their culinary skills to create a menu that features four seasonal changes.

The main floor dining room, with lead-glassed windows and doors, projects a classy image and the food served here follows suit.

The Kirk family is also very proud of what they've created in the lower level … a full-blown Bourbon Bar.

"We have at last count more than 360 bourbons," Larry Kirk says. "That makes us number one in the world. I think one in Louisville has 160."

Four Roses Distillery named the Miller House as one of the top 55 Bourbon Bars in America, and Kasey is turning out more of her unique dishes with an emphasis on bourbon.

From the fried green tomatoes, to the lobster rolls to the fried grit sticks to get things started, and then to a selection of beef dishes, pork chops, seafood, and chicken, this restaurant is top shelf.

You've got to try the meatloaf. Served with Yukon Gold mashed potatoes and sautéed green beans, it doesn't get any better than this. If you don't order it, see that someone else at your table does so you can have a taste.

Sunday brunch is available from 10 a.m. til 2 p.m., and has a kid's friendly menu.

DINERS INFORMATION

Address:
301 E. 5th Street
Hours:
Tuesday-Friday, 11 a.m. – 2 p.m. (Lunch)
Tuesday-Thursday, 5 p.m. – 9 p.m. (Dinner)
Friday-Saturday 5 p.m. – 10 p.m.
Sunday Brunch 10 a.m. – 2 p.m.
Tuesday-Saturday Bar, 4 p.m. – close
Phone:
270-685-5878
Price Range: $$
Area Attractions:
Bluegrass Music, Riverfront, Museum of Fine Art, Kentucky Wesleyan College

Mugsy's Hideout

MURRAY, KENTUCKY

Maybe there was a time when a restaurant named Mugsy's seemed out of place in Murray, Kentucky, but not any longer.

When Jay Baron and his wife, Maria, decided Murray was where they wanted to make their home after several visits to the lake area, the two Chicagoan's appropriately opened Mugsy's Hideout in downtown Murray in 2004.

With a passion for cooking, they've turned a dream into a reality, and no one is hiding out.

What would Mugsy's be without a Chicago-style hot dog, Polish and Italian sausage or a Mama Maria's meatball?

Pasta has its place, too, including spaghetti, baked mostaccoli, and chicken parmesan. The latter two feature penne pasta. A variety of offerings listed include a beer battered cold water cod fish, dressed with lettuce, tomato, and tartar sauce served on a roll.

Salads, and of course, pizzas are

served. There's the thin crust, but the real attention getter at Mugsy's is the deep dish. It takes a bit more time, so have a little patience when ordering.

There's another menu item you might want to take a serious look at. Italian Beef! Jay says he uses a three day process to prepare the beef ... I'll try to explain it. Here goes ... well, let Jay tell you when you eat there. Know this for sure, it's slow roasted, thinly sliced, and served on a roll with a side cup of au jus for nifty dipping.

Mugsy's has a limited bar with beer, wine, and a few bourbons.

DINERS INFORMATION

Address:
410 Main Street
Hours:
Tuesday-Friday, 11 a.m. – 8 p.m.
Saturday, 12 noon – 8 p.m.
Closed Sunday and Monday
Phone:
270-767-0020
Price Range: $$
Area Attractions:
Murray State University, Lakes

Parcell's Deli & Grill

BENTON, KENTUCKY

Parcell's is not in a historic building, nor does it have a beautiful view of the water, but what it does have is really, really good eats.

Located in a small shopping center, owner Daniel Slayden has managed over the last several years to expand from a few lunchtime sandwiches to dinner and a full-blown bakery.

"We strive to serve our customers the freshest selections possible," Daniel says.

From the looks of things it works, as customer's line up to place their orders.

Salads include grilled chicken, garden tuna, chicken salad, crispy chicken salad, and a chef salad. Also offered are a grilled chicken cordon bleu sandwich, grilled tenderloin sandwich, and a breaded tenderloin (cracker-crumb seasoning and fried to a juicy golden brown).

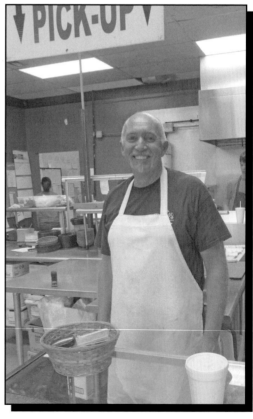

There are 10 different ways you can get a burger at Parcell's, and all of these specialty burgers are double meat and double cheese. Are you kidding me?

All of the deli sandwiches are served on fresh baked buns of rye, white or whole wheat.

You can choose from turkey club, smoked turkey breast, white tuna salad, California chicken salad or egg salad. Rueben's, grilled cheese, ham and cheese, BLT, and even a peanut butter and jelly are there for the choosing.

An interesting sidebar to Parcells Deli and Grill is that if you go to the bakery, you stroll through a wonderful little gift shop called Diedra's Market Place. They are all connected for a unique experience.

Address:
165 U.S. Hwy. 68E Draffenville Plaza
Hours:
Monday-Thursday, Open 10:30 a.m. — 8 p.m. (Summer)
Friday-Saturday, 10:30 a.m. — 9 p.m.
Closed Sunday
Bakery opens at 5 a.m. — 7 days a week
Phone:
270-527-9300
Price Range: $$
Area Attractions:
Lakes, fishing

47

Reva's Place

CADIZ, KENTUCKY

Forget the Cadiz by-pass. The next time you're there, take the scenic Main Street route through town, and right there in the middle of town is Reva's at the corner of Main and Marion.

This is a breakfast and lunch eatery, except on Friday's and Saturdays when they pack em' in for dinner.

Breakfast is a home cooking delight with, of course, eggs, hash browns, bacon, sausage, gravy, country ham, and an assortment of breakfast sandwiches. And what would a breakfast be at Reva's without omelets.

The lunches and dinners feature buffets that often include farm raised catfish and cod.

For those not wanting the buffet, a dinner menu has ribeyes, chicken tenders, fried jumbo shrimp, catfish, grilled chicken and country fried steak. A children's menu is also available.

Burgers, BLT's, clubs, grilled cheese and a delicious open faced roast beef sandwich with mashed potatoes and gravy are all popular here.

While waiting for a table in the 60-seat restaurant, an open doorway leads to a small shop that features local artists and artisans.

Address:
65B Main Street
Hours:
Sunday-Thursday, 7 a.m. — 2 p.m.
Friday-Saturday, 7 a.m. — 8 p.m.
Closed Sunday
Phone:
270-522-0806
Price Range: $
Area Attractions:
Lake Barkley, arts & crafts and antiques

Rookies Food & Spirits

HENDERSON, KENTUCKY

Rookies Food and Spirits calls itself a sports bar. And with 36 TV's, a bar area that seats 90, and an additional 150 in the dining room, no one will argue the point.

But the food here is far more sophisticated than the name. Sure, they've got the typical assortment of bar foods, like the fried green tomatoes, nachos, quesadilla, and cheese sticks, but it's their steaks that are Rookie's star attraction.

"The beef is our signature item," owner Rodney Thomas says. "It's all certified Angus."

From ribeyes to filet mignon to the flat iron, a steak here will be remembered.

Teriyaki chicken, spaghetti, pork tenderloin, Woodford Reserve salmon, shrimp and crab tortellini, and catfish all add to the unexpected choices visitors will have in this sports bar. And almost out of nowhere comes a

salad called Arabian Salad. Wow! Crisp greens, peppers, tomatoes, onions, tossed with a lemon-herb dressing, it is served with tasty unleavened bread.

Rookies has been around since 1984 when Rodney's dad, Fred, got it going. There's also a banquet area that can seat another 150 customers.

When you go, take some time and check out the sports memorabilia that covers the walls.

Address:
117 2nd Street
Hours:
Monday-Saturday, 4 p.m. — 10 p.m.
Closed Sunday
Phone:
270-826-1106
Price Range: $$
Area Attractions:
W.C. Handy Music Festival, John James Audubon State Park

Short's Family Restaurant

Short's sits just off of the West Kentucky Parkway in Muhlenberg County … not particularly difficult to find. However, if you do make a wrong turn or two, have patience. It's worth it.

The structure has been a restaurant since sometime in the 60's, but since Paula and Bobby Short took it over, it has continued to get better and better.

Breakfast begins here at 6 a.m., with a full menu that you would expect at a good affordable restaurant. Eggs, bacon, sausage, country ham, biscuits & gravy, pancakes, French toast, hash browns, omelets, on and on and on are staples at Short's.

A full complement of sandwiches highlights a menu that results in lots of decisions to make.

One of the big draws is the catfish dinner served on Thursday, Friday and Saturday nights.

Shirley Miller, who operates Short's on a daily basis, points out that the special buffets are a huge draw. One of those is the Saturday morn-

ing breakfast buffet from 6 a.m.–11 a.m., another is on Friday and Saturday nights from 4 p.m.–8 p.m., and then on Sundays from 11 a.m.–6 p.m.

Short's also has T-bone and ribeye steaks, salads, chicken, fried green tomatoes, chicken wings, soups, chili and pizzas.

Without a doubt, there is something for everyone at this country restaurant.

Short's Family Restaurant can and does handle big crowds. With a main room that seats some 55 people, a dining room off to the side can handle another 110.

There's even a walk-up dairy bar window that's part of the restaurant for those who want to drive-up grab a shake, sundae or ice cream cone.

DINERS INFORMATION

Address:
6195 U.S. Hwy. 62 West
Hours:
Monday-Tuesday, Thursday-Saturday, 6 a.m. – 8 p.m. (Summer)
Sunday, 7 a.m. – 8 p.m.
Closed on Wednesday
Phone:
270-338-7327
Price Range: $
Area Attractions:
Lake Malone

Wild Mountain Bakery & Café

MURRAY, KENTUCKY

Owner Karen Muse is quick to say, "Our cinnamon rolls are our signature item."

That might be because as soon as you step through the door the sweet, delicious aroma shouts, "you can't leave here without one … or two … or three."

Wild Mountain, though, is about a lot of good eats. Their doors open at 6 a.m., and quickly their egg bagel sandwiches start to go. With several options of breakfast sandwiches, as well as French baguette and other artisan breads, it's easy to see why this order-at-the-counter downtown Murray café has become so popular.

Lunch here is special, too. With such sandwich names as Smoke Bomb Turkey (turkey, bacon, smoked Gouda and a spicy chipotle sauce), and Mountain Man (corn beef, roast beef, turkey, chipotle mayo and Karen's special sauce), this place offers a presentation of lunch choices not found just anywhere in Murray.

Vegetarian, Italian, Reuben, grilled cheese and salami and pepperoni are all a part of the mix at Wild Mountain.

This restaurant is equally known for its specialty drinks: coffees (latte, cappuccino, mocha, and espresso), hot tea, smoothies, and bottled drinks that include fruit juice.

And those desserts! They're made from scratch right there in the kitchen. Yes, the cinnamon rolls, brownies, cookies, cupcakes, muffins and cheesecake are all fresh.

DINERS INFORMATION

Address:
412 Main Street
Hours:
Tuesday-Saturday, 6 a.m. – 4 p.m.
Closed Sunday and Monday
Phone:
270-761-9453
Price Range: $
Area Attractions:
Murray State University, antiques, lakes

Bell House Restaurant	Shelbyville, KY
Bluebird Café	Stanford, KY
Bluegrass Pizza	Danville, KY
Brooks' General Store Café	Sonora, KY
Bub's Café	Elizabethtown, KY
Burke's Bakery	Danville, KY
Check's	Louisville, KY
Clay's Downtown	Paris, KY
Cobbler's Café	Elizabethtown, KY
Corner Café	Louisville, KY
Fava's Restaurant	Georgetown, KY
Isaac's Café	Clermont, KY
Jailhouse Pizza	Brandenburg, KY
JT's Pizza & Subs	Simpsonville, KY
Keeneland Track Kitchen	Lexington, KY
Laha's Red Castle	Hodgenville, KY
Laker Drive-In	Stephensburg, KY
Longhunters Coffee & Tea Company	Greensburg, KY
Mammy's	Bardstown, KY
Manny & Merle	Louisville, KY
Napa Prime	Versailles, KY
Office Pub & Deli	Frankfort, KY
Olde Bus Station	Harrodsburg, KY

CENTRAL REGION

Q & A Sweet Treats	LaGrange, KY
Rails Restaurant & Bar	LaGrange, KY
Red State BBQ	Lexington, KY
Ricardo's Grill & Pub	Versailles, KY
Shack in the Back BBQ	Fairdale, KY
Stinky and Coco's	Winchester, KY
Stull's Country Store	Payneville, KY
A.P. Suggins Bar & Grill	Lexington, KY
Wagner's Pharmacy	Louisville, KY

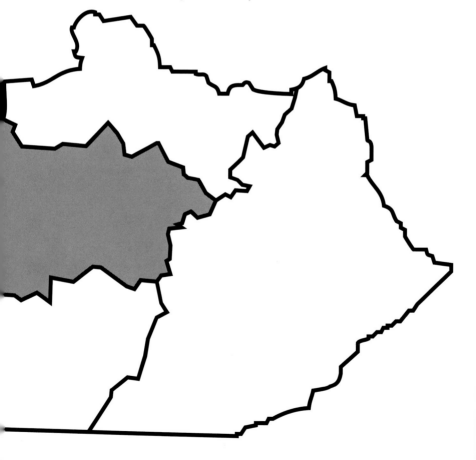

Bell House Restaurant

Bob and Sue Andriot, along with daughter Mary Miller, have one fine restaurant in Shelbyville, and since they opened have gained a regional reputation for wonderful eats in a great atmosphere.

The large four-room house in the heart of downtown was built in 1902, first as a residence before becoming an office to several businesses. Along the way, in 1950, the local firehouse underwent a renovation that involved getting rid of the large fire bell that sat atop of the firehouse in the town square, and the bell found its way to the front yard of the businesses at 721 Main Street. Then later, when Bob and Sue purchased the property and restored the old house into one of the best restaurants around, it was a no-brainer in what to call their place … The Bell House.

When looking at the menu, one quickly notices that it is not overpowering. In other words, there are not an overabundance of so many choices that is not only confusing to the customer, but the kitchen, too.

The Bell House does it just right. From the creamy tomato basil soup to the Isle of Capris Salad, to the delicious hot brown, to the Bell House chicken salad sandwich, all the way to the Henry Bain Pork or Béarnaise filet, this restaurant does it right.

The down home ambience of each room sets the tone for good conversation, friendly service and a memorable meal.

The Bell House's hours vary on weekends, six days a week it is basically a lunch spot, but the Friday and Saturday nights it brings out a top notch dinner menu that one would expect in a place like this.

Please be advised, if you are anywhere near Shelbyville, make your way to the Bell House.

DINERS INFORMATION

Address:
721 Main Street
Hours:
Monday-Saturday, 11 a.m. – 2:30 p.m.
Friday and Saturday (Italian Dining), 5 p.m. – 9 p.m. (Dinner)
Closed Sunday
Phone:
502-437-5678
Price Range: $$
Things of interest:
Horse farm tours, downtown shops, Outlet Mall, Shelbyville Horse Show

Bluebird Café

STANFORD, KENTUCKY

Right smack in the middle of this little central Kentucky town is one very fine restaurant that has turned out to be the catalyst of a tourism explosion.

Because of the Bluebird Café, it seems like everyone who hears about it wants to come and try it out.

Chef-owner Bill Hawkins has created a destination restaurant in a non-intimidating atmosphere that appeals not only to the locals, but also some of the so-called big-city-slickers. At the Bluebird, everything and everyone fits nicely together.

Chef Hawkins brings a history of food prep highlights that can and do stack up with the best in Kentucky. To Stanford he has brought his experiences of chef tenures at Florida golf resorts, Elvis Presley Enterprise on Beale Street in Memphis, to appearing on the Food Network with Bobby Flay, the Discovery Channel, and the Travel Channel.

"People ask me, 'Why Stanford?'," laughs Chef Hawkins. "It's easy. I had a chance to come to a place like this, and my family and I took it."

It seems that Jess and Angela Correll, who have helped to lead a resurgence in the downtown development of Stanford, set out to find a top-notch chef interested in getting involved in a farm-to-table high quality restaurant. They found Bill Hawkins.

"My mother was actually from this area of Kentucky, and when my wife and I came here to look around, we knew this was

it," he said. "I know, in a way, I'm an import, but we want to stay here. My mom told me if we do a good job, people will visit. She was right."

And visit they do.

This former grocery store building is now equipped with a kitchen that is open and visible from the tables and high back booths.

"I like it that people can see me working," he said. "We hide nothing."

The Bluebird tries to buy everything local. "We believe in small town local," Bill adds.

Breakfast is pretty much standard, if you call Amish eggs, served with homemade buttermilk biscuit and Markesbury Farm sausage gravy standard.

For lunch, try the fried green tomato BLT, and for dinner, well you can only imagine. Jambalaya, salmon mac & cheese, and weekly specials based on what ingredients are local, in season and available.

DINERS INFORMATION

Address:
202 West Main Street
Hours:
Monday-Thursday, 7:30 a.m. – 4 p.m.
Friday-Saturday, 7:30 a.m. – 9 p.m.
7:30 p.m. – 11 a.m. (Breakfast)
Phone:
606-365-1010
Price Range: $$
Area Attractions:
Shops

Bluegrass Pizza

DANVILLE, KENTUCKY

Colin Masters had a vision for a fun place to eat in downtown Danville. His first Bluegrass Pizza and Pub was a tad-bit too small, and his desire was something larger that would allow him to be more flexible in not only what he served, but also larger crowds.

He found that perfect location ... right across the street.

"We can seat 110, and have a full service bar and feature several craft beers that we brought to Danville," Colin says. "We're big enough now that we can take care of our locals, but also several of the visiting sports teams that come to Centre College."

Of course this charming, memorabilia laced eatery is all about pizzas, and Colin is proud of his two brick pizza ovens.

"Outside of Lexington, we're the only place in this area that has them," he says.

There's something else Colin likes to talk about and that's the quality of his food. "Some of it may be called bar food, but it's quality," he continues. "We raise all of the vegetables that we use on our farm. Our dough is also handmade."

The walls here are full of Colin's

rock 'n roll memorabilia and wife Melissa's photography. "I grew up in Louisville and enjoy music."

Bluegrass Pizza also has a menu full of sandwiches that include wraps, and pasta salads, cheese sticks, wings, fried pickles, bread sticks and salads.

One of the real kickers here is the "main line" pizza. It's a 4-pound pizza piled with pepperoni, Italian sausage, tomatoes, onions, green and black olives, fresh mushrooms and green peppers. There are others, too. With names like "mighty meat" and "Ms. Piggy" you can only imagine how large these are.

They have daily specials and Happy Hour from 3 p.m. – 6 p.m.

DINERS INFORMATION

Address:
314 W. Main Street
Hours:
Tuesday, 11 a.m. – 9 p.m.
Wednesday-Saturday, 11 a.m. – 10 p.m.
Closed Sunday and Monday
Phone:
859-236-7737
Price Range: $$
Area Attractions:
Centre College, Constitution Square, Brass Band Festival

Brook's General Store Café

The actual General Store here at Brook's is pretty much a thing of the past, but the Café part is going strong.

Delores Copelin and daughter Rhonda run the restaurant day-to-day, Monday through Friday.

"My parents, Ella Mae and Robert Brooks, started a grocery here in 1961," says Delores. "They lived in the same building, and when customers came in the store to buy groceries, they would smell my mom's home cooking."

Soon after the cooking part became full time and Brooks' was off and running as a place where the locals eat.

The sign hanging over the front of the building is a bit hard to read. Rusted, with the "r" in Brooks no longer there, it looks more like Books'.

"We actually have people that see the sign and come in looking for books," Rhonda laughed. "But that sign is so old, and it is a part of what we are that we decided to keep it like it is."

It just goes to prove that you don't need a big neon sign to get a customer, especially when the food is good.

Brooks' is a meat-and-two, plus cornbread place. With daily specials, meat loaf, mac & cheese, bar-b-que, chuck wagon, pork chops, real mashed potatoes and fried cornbread, this is a comfort food restaurant. And with nine sandwiches to choose from that include

burgers, ham, bologna, fish, bar-be-que, and chicken, there's something for everyone.

Desserts include homemade chocolate, peanut butter and coconut pies, and banana pudding round out some good home cooking.

Breakfast is also big at Brooks'. Biscuit and sausage gravy is one of the more popular items. Of course eggs, bacon, city ham, hash browns, sliced tomatoes and on and on are served from 8 a.m. – 10 a.m. only.

DINERS INFORMATION

Address:
135 Main Street
Hours:
Monday-Friday, 8:00 a.m. – 4:00 p.m.
Closed Saturday and Sunday
Phone:
270-369-8000
Price Range: $
Area Attractions:
Lincoln Birthplace, Lincoln Museum, antiques, Thurman-Phillips House (Charles P. Thurman, Innkeeper)

Bub's Café

S hirley Bailey and daughter, Sheila Cox, don't get carried away with an extensive menu at their shopping center restaurant called Bub's in E'town. They don't need to.

"We try to keep it simple," says Shirley. "What our customers want."

The name "Bub's" came about when Shirley's husband and his brother, who hadn't seen each other in years, on first encounter called each other Bub.

Bub's opens at 6 a.m. Monday through Saturday, usually to a packed house of locals for breakfast. Omelets (four kinds), country ham and eggs, pancakes, biscuits and gravy, and all of the trimmings you would expect with a good breakfast, are very popular. Large sausage patties are also in demand. "We get our sausage from Boone Meats in Bardstown," says Shirley.

Lunchtime is big here, too.

Serving seven different burgers, and thirteen sandwiches to choose from, as well as salads and low-cal plates, Bub's is able to get the crowd in and out.

Bub's has been located in what is referred to as the Roses Shopping Center, but officially called Helmwood Plaza, since 1997 and is a gathering spot for the locals.

Address:
Helmwood Plaza — 31-W North
Hours:
Monday-Friday, 6 a.m. — 3 p.m.
Saturday, 6 a.m. — 11 a.m.
Closed Sunday
Phone:
270-765-4202
Price Range: $
Area Attractions:
Swopes Car of Yesteryear Museum, Patton Museum, Lincoln Birthplace, Lincoln Museum, Bourbon Trail

Burke's Bakery

DANVILLE, KENTUCKY

"This place has a great reputation," one customer was heard to say while waiting for her order to be placed in one of the many white cardboard boxes on the counter of this Danville icon.

She was right, and you could taste that reputation in every bite.

Even though the word "delicatessen" has been added to some of their promotional material, make no mistake, Burke's is a bakery. Sure, you can pick up sandwiches "to-go" made from chicken salad, ham salad, pimento cheese, baked ham, bologna, but it's all of the other delicious sweet-stuff that carries the load.

This four-generation bakery is known far and wide, and from the time their doors open in the morning 'til the time they close, there is a steady stream of customers in and out the front door.

"We ship all over, all the way to California," says manager Patty Burke, who along with husband Joe now head up the operation.

If you can even imagine a sweet treat, Burke's probably makes it. German chocolate cakes, fudge cakes, coconut cakes, cream pies, fruit pies, breads, buns, rolls, cookies, coffee cakes, pastries, sweet rolls, and a list of donuts too many to mention here, makes this a destination stop-off in Central Kentucky.

"We're known for lots of things, but probably the best is our salt-rising bread, donuts, and gingerbread men," Patty says. "And our deli sandwiches are popular, too."

DINERS INFORMATION

Address:
121 W. Main Street
Hours:
Monday-Friday, 7 a.m. – 6 p.m.
Saturday, 7 a.m. – 5 p.m.
Sunday, 12 noon – 4 p.m.
Phone:
859-236-5661
Price Range: $
Area Attractions:
Centre College, Constitution Square, Brass Band Festival

69

Check's

Check's is legendary when it comes to Louisville eateries. But to be more precise, it's a family tradition that began in 1944 by Joe and Mary Murrow, then passed on to Dr. Tom and Cheri Murrow, and today run by son John Murrow.

Check's is your prototype neighborhood restaurant and bar in the Schnitzleburg part of Louisville, and if central casting is needed for a movie, they'd send in Check's.

Recently, John and his family renovated the spot, thus giving it a freshened look that has retained the charm from days gone by. The clean looking black and white checkered floors offers a welcoming feel when customers come through the front door, and they usually wait in line to step up and place their orders right next to the bar.

This is one very busy restaurant, but don't be turned off if the line backs up all the way to the front door. It moves quickly and the food arrives surprisingly fast. (The fried chicken takes a bit longer).

Check's is a fun place to eat and have an ice cold beer to go along with your chili.

This is one place that as a whole doesn't

change from one visit to the next. Dads bring their sons and daughters here, and when they are parents and grandparents they do the same.

"Check's is all about the food, and all of the familiar faces we see in here," said one customer, smiling while waiting to place her order. "I've been coming here all my life."

The daily specials, Salisbury steak, roast beef, grilled cheese, parmesan chicken, mac and cheese, brats, chicken salad, corn bread, pork tenderloin, and ribeye sandwiches, are just a few of the choices on the large menu boards near the cash register.

John Murrow is not one of those owners who sits at the bar and chats. On any given day he can be seen delivering orders, busing tables, or, well, just doing what needs to be done.

Address:
1101 E. Burnett Avenue (Germantown)
Hours:
Monday-Thursday, 11 a.m. – 9 p.m.
Friday-Saturday, 11 a.m. – late
Sunday, 12 noon
Phone:
502-637-9515
Price Range: $
Area Attractions:
Churchill Downs, Derby Museum

Clay's Downtown

The saying after our soldiers returned from WWII was, "How you gonna keep 'em down on the farm after they've seen Parie?" Of course they were talking about Paris, France, but in this case you can visit Paris, Kentucky and still stay down on the farm ... horse farms, that is.

Clay's Downtown eatery fits in nicely with many of the upscale Thoroughbred horse layouts in this Bourbon County seat that has one of the most impressive courthouses in Kentucky.

Owner Frank Clay is a descendent of Henry Clay, who was labeled as "the great compromiser," in earlier days. But one thing for sure is that there is no compromising when it comes to serving delicious food that he and his chef-wife Elizabeth painstakingly prepare.

Clay's Downtown is a fancy restaurant without all of the fancy prices.

"We do everything possible to serve the freshest of food possible," says Elizabeth. "We are involved in the Kentucky Proud programs, and our meats are the best ... they're from Critchfield. And our seafood is flown in fresh ... nothing frozen."

As one might expect in the middle of horse country, paintings by local artist line the walls and are for sale.

The menu includes appetizers, soups, and salads, of course, but they also serve a complement of dinner salads you can make a meal of (shrimp scampi

72

salad, teriyaki salmon salad, Clay's layered pea salad, grilled or fried chicken salad).

Burges, crab cakes, prime rib, and steaks of all kinds, pork chops and pasta dishes galore round out a solid list of offerings.

"The Clay's have been in Kentucky for more than 200 years," says Elizabeth, a master chef. "We have 200 years of our name on this restaurant, so we want to do it right."

There's a patio that seats 45 in addition to a full service bar.

Address:
730 Main Street
Hours:
Tuesday-Thursday, 1 a.m. – 9 p.m.
Friday-Saturday, 11 a.m. – 10 p.m.
Closed Sunday and Monday
Phone:
859-987-6000
Price Range: $$
Area Attractions:
Claiborne Horse Farm, Gentleman Distillery (next door) which is the first distillery in Bourbon County since 1919.

Cobbler's Café

ELIZABETHTOWN, KENTUCKY

With a name like this, you've got to think Cobbler's Café is all about … well, cobblers. But that's not necessarily so.

"At one time over history, this building was a very prominent shoe shop," says owner Jayme Burden. "So it just seemed like a natural when we opened it up in 2004."

The shotgun style building actually dates back to 1878 when it was a doctor's office, and some of the original sun baked bricks can still be seen in the café's main dining area. This structure has been home to several businesses over the last century-plus years, but right now it seems like a natural that it is turning out not only great peach, apple or blackberry cobbler, but tasty made-to-order breakfasts, salads, sandwiches and wraps for lunch.

"We're also known for our Specialty Coffee drinks," Jayme added.

Cobbler's Café is just off the downtown square across from the Justice Center, with easy-access parking beside the restaurant.

The breakfast menu is offered all day long. It includes

omelet choices, biscuit and gravy, French toast sticks, scones, muffins and pastries, and even a breakfast pizza.

A glass case displays several of the delicious bakery-type items served here.

There's also a kid's menu that offers a variety of choices.

DINERS INFORMATION

Address:
125 E. Dixie Avenue
Hours:
Monday-Saturday, 7:30 a.m. – 3 p.m.
Closed Sunday
Phone:
270-982-2233
Price Range: $
Area Attractions:
Sports Park, Ft. Knox, Lincoln's Birthplace, The Hardin County Historical Museum

Corner Café

The Corner Café used to be on a corner, but a long time ago it moved into bigger digs and today it's still the Corner Café, but not on a corner.

The Frederick family, Robert, Randy, Scott, Peggy and friend, Alice Bowling run this restaurant, and they do it right!

The best way to describe it is comfortable with really good eats. The half-circle padded booths, the cloth covered tables, and the just-right chatter from other customers is a good mix in this 140-seat restaurant that opened in 1985.

The Corner Café with its full service bar, extensive wine list, and 30-plus beer menu is a neighborhood favorite that draws its customers from all over the Louisville area.

Located in the suburb of Lyndon, this get-there-early-to-get-a-table spot features a menu with a Cajun influence.

"The Andouille stuffed chicken," is a favorite here," says Robert Frederick. "It's been on our menu for 30 years."

The blackened beef tenderloin or shrimp and grits add even more to the bayou choices, but this classy strip center restaurant also serves Tijuana eggrolls, crab cakes, New York subs, gourmet pizzas, assorted delicious pasta dishes, steaks, chops and even gyros.

The Fredericks have this restaurant covered. With Robert out front and Randy, Scott and Peggy handling chef duties, you can bet this is one place that is all about quality.

Check out the beautiful art on the walls. They are for sale.

Just when you think you can't eat any more, they mention their desserts. Can you say Godiva chocolate pie? How about Randy's bread pudding? Or cheesecake? Or carrot cake? Thought you could.

Address:
9307 New LaGrange Road (Whipps Mill Shopping Center)
Hours:
Monday-Friday, 11 a.m. – 9 p.m.
Saturday, 5 p.m. – 10 p.m.
Closed Sunday
Phone:
502-426-8119
Price Range: $$
Area Attractions:
Shopping, shopping and more shopping

Fava's Restaurant

GEORGETOWN, KENTUCKY

Since 1910, Fava's in downtown Georgetown has been serving good things to eat ever since Louie and Susie Bertolini Fava opened their doors. First, it was ice cream and candy before becoming the legendary restaurant it is today.

Now Fava's is operated by John Gruchow, and he hasn't missed a beat.

"I eat in here three or four times a week," one customer was heard saying.

It was easy to see why. The six-seat lunch counter plus multiple booths and tables is like Grand Central Station in a good way every day.

Fava's is one of the most continual restaurants in the same location in all of Kentucky, and because of that, the locals gather here for breakfast and often again at lunchtime.

This iconic eatery has even served as the caterer of choice for a pair of ABC television shows, Extreme Makeover Home Edition and Super Nanny.

John Gruchow is proud of the extensive offerings at Fava's.

A full complement of breakfast items are served from eggs, bacon, sausage, and hashbrowns, to country ham, pancakes, omelets, and biscuits & gravy.

Lunches include about every kind of sandwich imaginable as well as soups and salads.

Dinner at Fava's has it going on, too: Country ham, hamburger steak, open faced roast

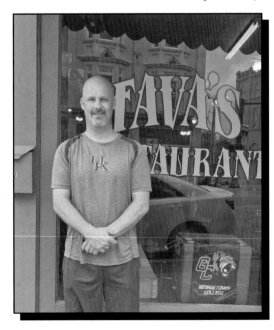

beef, pork tenderloin, catfish plate, grilled chicken breast platter and hot brown.

Friday and Saturday nights are really special. On these nights a rib-eye-shrimp combo dinner is served along with a jumbo shrimp platter, and shrimp-catfish dinner. These dinners include the salad bar.

"I try to buy locally," John adds. "This way what we turn out is as fresh as possible."

Desserts are traditional at Fava's: milkshakes, root beer floats, banana splits, hot fudge cake and homemade pies.

It's easy to see why Fava's has won numerous local restaurant awards.

DINERS INFORMATION

Address:
159 E. Main Street
Hours:
Monday-Saturday, 7 a.m. – 9 p.m.
Sunday, 10 a.m. – 3 p.m.
Phone:
502-863-4383
Price Range: $$
Area Attractions:
Georgetown College, Toyota Factory Tours, Horse Farms

Isaac's Café

CLERMONT, KENTUCKY

Isaac's Café may be the most unique restaurant in this book. Well, at least the setting. Not many are located in a beautiful forest … Bernheim Forest, not far from Shepherdsville in Bullitt County is one of the most beautiful places in Kentucky with its seasonal flower gardens, mirror-like lakes and numerous hiking trails.

And now adding to it all is Isaac's Café, named after Isaac Bernheim.

Pretty much a middle-of-the day café, Isaac's is all about eating healthy and doing so with locally grown food.

"We harvest our own food right here in our edible garden," manager Debbie Midgett says. "And what we don't do here we buy nearby."

The beef products come from Boone's Butcher Shop in Bardstown, and all of Isaac's cheese products come from well-known Kenny's Farm

House Cheeses in Barren County.

"We offer a Spring-Summer menu and a Fall-Winter one," Debbie adds. "And when we don't have fresh tomatoes we don't serve any. No grocery bought items here."

The most popular item here is the Nutty Bird sandwich. What a sandwich. This is easily a sandwich for two. Served on sun dried tomato bread, topped with layers and layers of turkey, followed by lettuce, bacon, and Norwood cheese and

sunflower seeds. All of this is then covered in a spicy bistro sauce, with a stack of home grown pickles on the side.

Locally grown vegetables make up the Leapin' Veggie Burger, with produce from Flying Leap Farm. Layered on a fresh Kaiser roll and topped with fresh greens and veggies from the garden as they ripen, the sandwich is then drizzled with a sweet Bourbon peach glaze.

A house-made chicken salad sandwich is another great choice. Soups, salads, cakes and pies are also offered. Save room for the ice cream.

DINERS INFORMATION

Address:
Hwy. 245, Clermont, KY
Hours:
Monday-Sunday, 11 a.m. — 4 p.m.
Closed major holidays
Phone:
502-955-8512, ext. 222
Price Range: $
Area Attractions:
Bernheim Forest, Jim Beam Distillery

Jailhouse Pizza

BRANDENBURG, KENTUCKY

You don't have to be locked up to eat here, but you can be if you want to.

You guessed it. Jailhouse Pizza is an old, historic jail that was built in 1906 and operated until 1976, until recycled into an eatery with a fantastic view of river traffic on the Ohio River either from inside, or out on the deck.

The pizza is good, especially the Baked Spaghetti and Philly Cheese Pizzas. But this restaurant, regardless of the name is much more than pizzas.

Lasagna, alfredo, sandwiches like Italian, meatball and chicken, chips and queso, garlic knots, salads, Stromboli's, calzones, wings, fried pickles, are just some of the selections you'll find here.

If you're really hungry, you might want to attempt the "Prisoners Pardon Pizza Challenge". It's for two. The two of you have 60 minutes to eat a

12-pound pizza. It's free if you do it, but you need to know that according to manager, Anita Overstreet, over 70 duos have attempted the feat, but none have succeeded. Heck, even if you don't you still get a T-shirt.

Part of the attraction here is the old jail itself. The individual cells have tables and chairs for dining, and a self-guided tour reveals an area where men were housed, and a separate area for women. There's even an area where hangings took place. Notice the trap door in the floor. Watch out!

One of the most notable prisoners was Hank Williams, Sr. Other historic figures who traveled through Brandenburg, but weren't jailed even though they probably should have been were John Hunt Morgan, and outlaws Jesse and Frank James.

DINERS INFORMATION

Address:
125 Main Street
Hours:
Tuesday-Thursday, 4 p.m. — 9 p.m.
Friday-Saturday, 11 a.m. — 10 p.m.
Sunday, 12 noon — 8 p.m.
Closed Monday
Phone:
270-422-4660
Price Range: $$
Area Attractions:
Ohio River, Otter Creek Park, Patton Museum

JT's Pizza & Subs

Often times shopping center restaurants are overlooked by the traveling public because of … well, because they are in shopping centers. Sure enough J.T.'s Pizza and Subs is one of them, but know this, this restaurant is not overlooked by the locals in Shelby County.

There's nothing fancy about this 100-seat spot with a small bar in the corner, but it doesn't need to be when usually there's nothing fancy about pizzas, subs, lasagna and spaghetti dishes.

"We keep our food fresh and simple, says manager Erika Green. "And our hot subs are really special."

She's right about that. These piled high sandwiches consisting of ham & turkey, ham & cheese, BLT, veggie, hot Sicilian, Italian, Stromboli, and meatball are all what helped put J.T.'s on the local food map and have kept it there.

Owner Joe Pendergest features several chalkboard daily specials consisting of subs or pizza or lasagna between 11 a.m. and 2 p.m., and then

for the evening meal, between 4 p.m. and 10 p.m., there are more specials for each day.

While pizza and subs are the big draw, it's the different specialty pizza combos that separate J.T.'s from the others.

"We hand toss each pizza with dough made fresh daily," Erika adds. "We use high quality ingredients,"

Behind the eight-seat bar, the wall is full of photos mostly of Seven Mary Three Band.

"Joe and I really like their music and follow them when we can wherever they play," Erika said.

For sure the "picture gallery" is a conversation piece, but so is the good food served here.

Address:
129 Buck Creek Road (Simpsonville Towne Centre)
Hours:
Monday-Saturday, 11 a.m. – 10 p.m.
Closed Sunday
Phone:
502-722-9030
Price Range: $
Area Attractions:
Horse farm tours, Shelbyville Horse Show, Metzger's Country Store, Outlet Mall

Keeneland Track Kitchen

For the most part, the general public is unaware that the Track Kitchen located on the grounds of this National Historic Landmark horse track is open to "outsiders," but it is.

"We've had a track kitchen here for 75 years, although not in this exact location," says manager Pete Kelder. "We serve good hearty food at reasonable prices."

Because it's Keeneland, customers might be dining with exercise riders, hot walkers, jockeys, trainers and even owners.

"The thing about a track kitchen is you might have someone who cleans out stalls sitting next to an owner worth a $100 million dollars," Kelder says. "That's the nature of horse tracks."

Much of the allure is the Keeneland grounds as you drive through, past the track on your left, the sales pavilion on the right, by the horse barns before reaching Track Kitchen Drive where the restaurant is located. A suggestion is to follow the signs carefully.

To eat here you do not have to have a race ticket. Enter the main entrance off of Versailles Road across from the airport.

As expected, breakfast is standard morning food … eggs, bacon, sausage, biscuits,

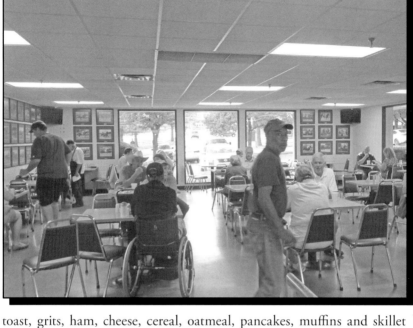

toast, grits, ham, cheese, cereal, oatmeal, pancakes, muffins and skillet potatoes. Cafeteria-style is the way the food is served, and by all means do not pass up the biscuits and gravy.

The enthusiasm of the servers does not go unnoticed, and one of them proudly proclaims that they are told by "horse people", that this is the cleanest track kitchen in the country.

There are three different times during the year the Track Kitchen changes its hours of operation. When racing is going on, the hours are 5 a.m. to 7 p.m.; Keeneland sales 5 a.m. to 5 p.m.; regular hours 6 a.m. to 11 a.m. daily.

DINERS INFORMATION ?

Address:
4201 Versailles Road
Hours:
Monday-Sunday, 6 a.m. – 11 a.m.
Keeneland sales, 5 a.m. – 5 p.m.
During racing, 5 a.m. – 7 p.m.
Phone:
859-254-3412 ext. 4896
Price Range: $
Area Attractions:
Keeneland Race Track, Kentucky Horse Park, UK sports

Laha's Red Castle

HODGENVILLE, KENTUCKY

In 1934, William and Sally Laha started selling hamburgers out of a little walkup on the square in Hodgenvillle. All the years later, Laha's Red Castle is still selling burgers, but now inside.

"White Castle was already established when my husband's grandparents opened here and they decided to call theirs Red Castle," Anita Laha laughed.

Food life is relatively simple at Laha's. The burgers and chili dogs are served on wax paper, drinks out of cans, or little glass bottles of Coke. The only seating includes 10 stools at a counter that sits in front of a large Vulcan grill that was installed in the 1950's.

Four to five full time employees wearing red Laha T-shirts are in continuous motion cranking out double cheese burgers, chili, chili dogs, on-

88

ion rings, not just for the customers inside but for numerous carry-out orders. This is one busy place.

"I'll have a diet Pepsi," shouted one customer, "And throw down some fries with that, please."

Laha's is an institution in Hodgenville. Lots of tourists come to town to visit Lincoln's Birthplace, and many of them ask about where to eat? Laha's pops up, so the parking spots

near the eatery are occupied by out of town cars, whose occupants are enjoying some of their hand-made fresh hamburgers.

"We served five or six generations of customers," says Anita, who along with husband Kelly is never far from the business. "And our son Ethan, who works here sometimes, is a fourth generation Laha."

In a bit of an oddity, Laha's closes at 1:30 p.m. on Wednesday's. "It used to be years ago that the banks and court house here closed at 1:30 on Wednesday," Anita offered. "So, we just stayed with the tradition."

DINERS INFORMATION

Address:
21 Public Square
Hours:
Monday-Saturday, 9 a.m. – 4 p.m.
Wednesday, 9 a.m. – 1:30 p.m.
Phone:
270-358-9201
Price Range: $
Area Attractions:
Lincoln Birthplace, Lincoln Museum, Lincoln Boyhood Home, Lincoln Jamboree

89

Laker Drive-In

STEPHENSBURG, KENTUCKY

"You can't believe all of the people who call us and ask what movie we have playing tonight," laughs owner-manager Kaylyn Bowen. "They think because of our name we're a drive-in movie."

There may not be anything on a big screen here, but what is playing is plenty of good food that customers line up for at this walk-up restaurant that first opened in 1964.

"Darold and Olene Richardson opened it, and when my parents, Michelle and John Bowen, took over several years ago we kept everything the same," Kaylyn says.

You don't walk up here, order your food and they hand it to you. No sir, you order it and they cook-to-order. There's usually a short wait, but they call your name over a loud speaker so you can hear it if you're sitting in your car.

It's busy here, so don't be in a real big hurry.

The name Laker came from the old nearby West Hardin High School that is now a middle school. The nickname of their sports teams was the Lakers.

Laker Drive-In is known for a lot of good food, but at the top of the list is the Lakerburger, that stars two burgers on a three layer bun with cheese, lettuce, tomato, pickle, onion, tartar sauce and their own special sauce added to that. You can be sure this is not a one-hand sandwich. And also be sure to get a couple of extra napkins. Yes, it's that good.

Close behind on the popularity list are the chuckwagon and tenderloin sandwiches, followed by the onion rings.

Foot long chili dogs are high on the list. So, too, are the milkshakes. Can you say peanut butter milkshake? You won't regret it.

DINERS INFORMATION

Address:
10585 Leitchfield Road (Hwy. 62 approximately 8 miles from E'town)
Hours:
Monday-Saturday, 10:30 a.m. – 9 p.m.
Sunday, 12 noon – 9 p.m.
Winter time hours, usually November, close at 8 p.m.
Phone:
270-862-4183
Price Range: $
Areas of Interest:
Lincoln Birthplace

Longhunters Coffee & Tea Company

GREENSBURG, KENTUCKY

When Bill and Justine Landrum decided to move back to their family roots a few years ago and open up a restaurant in Greensburg, they did it right.

Taking an old historic downtown building and turning it into a destination restaurant in the area means that the locals don't have to drive, and drive and drive to celebrate a special occasion. But that doesn't mean Longhunters is a high-hat place either. It has the ambiance of a history museum (which it really does have on the second floor), while at the same time offering a menu of hot browns, hearty sandwiches and fresh plated salads. Many of the offerings are named after famous Green County citizens who became a part of early-day American history.

"We wanted to do something nice here," offered Bill Landrum in somewhat of an understatement.

Longhunters serves breakfast, too: crepes in an assortment of flavors, as well as delicious sausage gravy and biscuits, pancakes and French toast that is baked with ground cinnamon and stuffed with strawberries and cream cheese and then dusted with powdered sugar. Of course, eggs, bacon and pancakes can be ordered.

Now, let's get to the coffees and teas, after all, it's part of the Longhunters name. Mocha, latte, flavored brews, cappuccino and espresso, served regular or

92

iced, are what separates this restaurant from others in the area. And Bill says the hot herbal teas served here can be addictive.

For really something special, if you can get here on Sunday, a full brunch buffet is served. Wow! Scrambled eggs, sausage, bacon, biscuit & gravy, corn fritters, mashed red-skin potatoes, waffles, French toast, and pork chops, finished off with carrot or Italian cream cake are some of the selections.

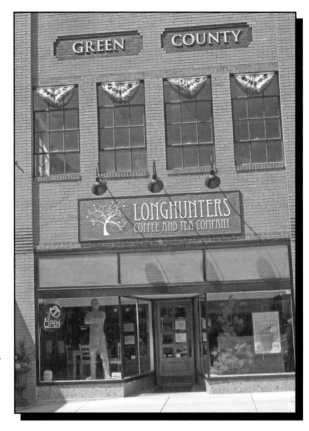

What the Landrums have done with their restaurant compliments a scenic historic downtown Greensburg. Bring your camera.

DINERS INFORMATION

Address:
115 South Public Square
Hours:
Monday-Thursday, 8 a.m. – 2 p.m.
Friday-Saturday, 8 a.m. – 7 p.m.
Sunday Brunch, 10:30 a.m. – 1 p.m.
Phone:
270-932-2351
Price Range: $$
Area Attractions:
Museum, Historic Court House, old walking bridge, Ski (soft drink) Bottling Company

Mammy's

BARDSTOWN, KENTUCKY

What started out in 2006 as a combination café, antique and sewing store, has now evolved into an almost 200-seat restaurant in the heart of downtown Bardstown.

"I don't know how we did it," says owner Christy Clark about those early years. "We've now moved four times, all downtown, to get to where we are."

Mammy's name came from Christy's two grandmothers, one who had 17 children and the other 15. With that said, you just know home cookin' was big in these two families … real big!

Today, that kitchen has been passed down to this popular Nelson County eatery.

Christy, husband Daniel, and daughter Robyn, get each day started with a full blown breakfast menu that they'll fix just about any way or any combination you want.

From salads to soups to sandwiches that include chicken, fish, ribeye, Rueben's, burgers, bourbon dogs (covered in a bourbon sauce and topped with onion tanglers and Swiss cheese).

After 5 p.m., Mammy's rolls out their dinner specials. Some of them are country fried or pulled pork chops, chicken, country ham, ribeye steaks and catfish.

Almost every day there's a different special that keeps the locals coming back, sometimes twice a day.

Mondays and Saturdays are usu-

94

ally meatloaf days, open-faced roast beef is Tuesday, and Friday is fried chicken day.

As might be expected here, the desserts are homemade.

There's also a popular bar area that extends outside to an inviting fireplace.

Address:
116 W. Stephen Foster
Hours:
Monday-Saturday, 6:30 a.m. – 11 a.m. (Breakfast)
Monday, 11 a.m. – 3 p.m. (Lunch)
Tuesday-Saturday, 11 a.m. – 9 p.m. (Lunch-Dinner)
Sunday, 8 a.m. – 2 p.m. (Breakfast-Lunch)
Phone:
502-350-1097
Price Range: $
Area Attractions:
Bourbon Trail, My Old Kentucky Home, Oscar Getz Whiskey Museum

Manny and Merle

Most of the time there's a story behind the name of a restaurant, and this Whiskey Row spot is no exception.

"Manny is our cook here who has been with us a long time," says Judy Palombino, who along with husband Tony are the proprietors. "And Merle comes from Merle Haggard and the songs he sings.

This is one unique place. It's all about a good time, and it is a self-described "honky tonk." Live entertainment plays on the weekend, but even when the jukebox type music shouts out "here's a quarter ... call someone who cares," customers know they're not in a typical restaurant.

The food is of Mexican influence with tortilla soup, house made chips and salsa, queso and pretzels, black beans, salads, sandwiches (queso burger, roast pork, carne or pollo asada), and mega choice of tacos.

Whiskey Row is the appropriate location for Manny and Merle, especially when you consider the food selections that accompany the margaritas, sangria and shots of bourbon and tequila. Oh yes, and the cold beer of which there are more than 20 to choose from.

Manny and Merle is unique in that it has proven that even with the popularity of all of the Kentucky bourbons, tequila here has managed to hold its own. In fact, just as bourbon flights are offered, so, too, are tequila flights.

But let's get back to those tacos. The brisket taco is slow braised beef, caramelized onions and peppers, cilantro and queso fresco. And then there's the green chili pork taco. This is where you might want to go ahead and order a cold beer before it arrives. Pulled pork, green chili jam, roasted garlic crema and cilantro are combined to create this show stopper. "When it's gone you are sad," says Alli, one of the wait staff here.

Judy and Tony have done a great job in taking this old downtown building and restoring the interior to match the music, creative bar menu and legendary bourbons and tequilas.

DINERS INFORMATION

Address:
122 W. Main Street
Hours:
Tuesday-Thursday, 11 a.m. – 11 p.m.
Friday, 11 a.m. – 2 a.m.
Saturday, 4 p.m. – 2 a.m.
Closed Sunday and Monday
Phone:
502-290-8888
Price Range: $
Area Attractions:
Louisville Slugger Museum, Mohammad Ali Center, Yum Center

Napa Prime

Just because this eatery is located in what used to be a chain restaurant, don't let the lack of a fancy façade keep you from stopping in. This little place is really good.

Chef-owner Darrell Lewis and his wife Lori have figured it out. Serve really good food and the people will come.

"We think our name, Napa Prime, stands for quality, and that's what we are all about," Lori says. "We love wine and quality food."

Although there is a lack of a bar presence here, customers can still get adult beverages that do indeed include wine.

Darrell has a vast assortment of menu items he list under a "handheld" heading, and it starts with just maybe the best fish tacos you've ever tasted. With tempura battered fish combined with their special Napa slaw, Pico de Gallo and srircha aioli, all inside of a crisp taco shell, make this one of the more popular items here. There's also a hangover burger that includes bacon, cheese and a fried egg. And then, how about a lamb burger with Greek feta cheese, baby spinach, pickled red onions and a red wine jam sauce?

Under the "knife & fork" heading are several chicken dishes, and seafood driven dishes that include truffled crab mac & cheese, shrimp diablo penne, and pan seared salmon. There's also meatloaf, pork chops and ribeyes.

Of course there are appetizers. But there's one in particular you've got to try. You may not have ordered it without reading about it in this book. It's the loaded tater tots. Yes, tater tots, prepared crispy brown with a loaded truffle fondue cheese sauce. Four people can enjoy this out-of-nowhere-treat.

Napa Prime has a nice selection for the kids. There's not an abundance of dessert offerings, but there really doesn't need to be when you've got bourbon caramel bread pudding with a scoop of vanilla ice cream on top. Get an extra spoon.

Address:
508 Lexington Road
Hours:
Monday-Saturday, 11 a.m. – 10 p.m.
Sunday, 10 a.m. – 9 p.m. (brunch served 10 a.m. – 2 p.m.)
Phone:
859-873-0600
Price Range: $$

Office Pub & Deli

FRANKFORT, KENTUCKY

Ever since this restaurant opened its doors in 1979, it has been one of those iconic places where people went to be seen and to not be seen in Kentucky's capitol city. You can only guess what stories might come out if these walls could talk.

The Office Pub and Deli is believed to be the oldest continuing family restaurant in Frankfort, and owner John Presley very well might be the most accommodating restaurateur in all of Kentucky.

"We'll try to serve anything our customer wants if we have the ingredients," Presley says. "They just have to ask and we'll do our best."

If it's been awhile since you've been to the Office Pub, there's still a good chance it looks like it did when you were last here. That's the allure of this legendary restaurant.

Though the inside hasn't changed much over the years, you can bet the menu has definitely kept up with the times.

"Our menu is the most diverse in Frankfort," Presley adds. "We have a loyal local clientele that appreciates the quality of our food. We use only fresh and locally cut steaks, and prefer locally grown vegetables."

Appetizers include onion straws, Italian breaded cheese sticks, pickle chips and fried green tomatoes. Soups and salads are served with delicious griddle fried cornbread.

"We're a cheers type place," offered one customer, taking ownership because she is a regular here.

There's a multitude of ways customers can order their burgers, but one thing for sure is they are 100% Black Angus beef.

All kinds of sandwiches are served … chicken, fish, turkey, Reuben, BLT, pork tenderloin, chuckwagon, and bar-b-que.

The Office Pub, according to Presley, is the only restaurant in the area to serve lamb fries.

The Office Pub & Deli has several big screen TV's for special sporting events, and when the Cats are playing an in-house speaker system broadcast the games loud and clear.

DINERS INFORMATION

Address:
614 Comanche Trail
Hours:
Monday-Thursday, 11 a.m. – 10 p.m.
Friday and Saturday, 11 a.m. – 11 p.m.
Closed Sunday
Phone:
502-227-9585
Price Range: $$
Area Attractions:
Kentucky State Capitol, Kentucky Vietnam Veterans Memorial

Olde Bus Station

HARRODSBURG, KENTUCKY

The inside of the Olde Bus Station Restaurant looks like ... well, what an old Greyhound bus station looked like.

"That's what it was beginning in the early 1940's," says owner Lora White. "And that's the way it stayed until they stopped running here in 1991."

Today about all that's original are the hardwood floors. But Lora has a few of the "back-in-the-day" old black and white photos of the station.

During the week, this spot is all about breakfast and lunch, featuring a full morning compliment of food that spills over into lunch time, and the "lunch plate specials" as well as salads, Philly steaks, grilled ham and Swiss, BLT's, and chicken melts. Burgers with names that pay homage to local high school nicknames have their place on the menu, too.

Desserts are very popular here.

"One of the first jobs that I had was working in a restaurant here in Har-

rodsburg," says Lora. "I was 14 and my job was to make the ice cream. So when I opened here I knew I had to make the homemade banana ice cream. I remembered the recipe."

The Olde Bus Station seats close to 60 people inside, including nine stools at the counter. A few years ago a covered outside deck was added that handles another 50.

Weekends have extended hours on Friday night. "We serve all-you-can-eat catfish on Friday nights," Lora said.

Address:
227 S. Greenville Street
Hours:
Monday-Thursday, 6 a.m. – 2 p.m.
Friday, 6 a.m. – 8 p.m.
Saturday, 8 a.m. – 2 p.m.
Sunday, 11 a.m. – 2 p.m.
Phone:
859-734-4202
Price Range: $
Area Attractions:
Shaker Village at Pleasant Hill, Fort Harrod, History

Q & A Sweet Treats

Several years ago, Andrea Essenpries took the advice of family and friends and hasn't looked back.

"I was selling cookies and other baked goods at our Farmers Market, and they said I should open up a bakery and sell them all the time," said Andrea.

And she did.

That was in 2011, and now she is turning out sweetness classics in the form artisan breads (honey wheat, olive Rosemary, and cinnamon swirl to name a few); scones (blueberry, apricot, raspberry, and cranberry orange); cookies (sugar, double chocolate chip, molasses spice, peanut butter, snickerdoodle, and white chocolate coconut); whoopee pies, and brownies. Oh yes … about those brownies. "Each batch begins with 2 ½ pounds of premium semisweet chocolate and two pounds of creamery butter," says Andrea. "We don't skimp on quality."

Q & A turns out lots of specialty items, too … hand decorated cakes and cookies. One of those cookies is called "Black & White." One half is chocolate icing, and the other half vanilla.

Located in an old house, Andrea wanted more than just paint on the walls, so she has decorated some with photos of some of the local kids who have been customers over the years.

"They'll love coming back and seeing them when they grow up," she added.

Several table and chairs create a comfortable relaxed atmosphere that customers can utilize while enjoying a cup of custom blended coffee and a baked treat.

And what about the Q & A name? "Well, the Q came from a former cookie company called "Q" and I added the "A" for Andrea," she said.

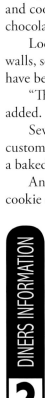

DINERS INFORMATION

Address:
211 S. First Street
Hours:
Tuesday-Friday, 7 a.m. — 6 p.m.
Saturday, 8 a.m. — 2 p.m.
Closed Sunday and Monday
Phone:
502-265-0550
Price Range: $$
Area Attractions:
Farm tours, trains, shops

Rails Restaurant & Bar

LAGRANGE, KENTUCKY

Owner Ellie Troutman is all about farm to table and buying locally. And her menu proves it.

This sophisticated eatery offers dishes that are not often served in smaller towns.

If you've been to LaGrange, you know that the train tracks run right through the middle of town. It's really what makes this charming downtown so unique. A train only a few feet away has become a part of the landscape … at least several times a day.

The bison burgers and steaks are locally raised, as are the lamb selections.

At night, Rails takes on an elegant setting with white tablecloths and black napkins and when each dish arrives at your table the chef has created a presentation that matches the surroundings.

The Caprese salad is a knockout. Heirloom tomatoes, buffalo mozzarella, basil, olive oil and a balsamic vinegar reduction make this a good way to start any dining experience.

One of the lunch items is the steak chimichurri, a 6-ounce Kentucky Proud grilled grass-fed flank steak, and then served with Rails homemade chimichurri sauce. A larger portion is offered for dinner.

Rails beef Wellington is beef tenderloin wrapped in a homemade puff pastry with foie gras, mushroom and wine sauce that is then baked.

The lamb empanadas are another puff pastry offering, albeit an appetizer. The lamb is prepared with olives, tomatoes, red wine, peppers and onions and served with a meat sauce.

The menu offers seafood, pastas, sandwiches and some pretty flashy desserts, as you would expect from a restaurant of this caliber.

DINERS INFORMATION

Address:
117 E. Main
Hours:
Sunday-Saturday, 11 a.m. – 9 p.m.
Phone:
502-225-6622
Price Range: $$
Area Attractions:
Trains, antique shops, Farm tours

Red State BBQ

By its own admission, this is a barbeque joint. But before it became one of the best "cue" restaurants around, the building was a restaurant for the still existing Sunset Motel that sits outback.

Owned by David Carroll, the name Red State BBQ came about as an offhand comment between friends. While watching the election returns one night, Scott Ahlschwede, the original owner, turned to a friend and said, "You ever notice how all the good barbecue comes from the red states?" The rest is history, and today this is one busy restaurant with some very big servings of food.

Manager Tony Selby is a whirlwind of activity, while making sure no one leaves Red State hungry.

It can start with their Frickles pickles fried in a light beer batter made from a local beer, or beer cheese served with soft pretzels. Speaking of beer cheese, Red State has figured out a couple of ways to combo it with their brisket and beer cheese grits.

You have never seen such a serving of pulled pork between two buns. And then there are the ribs. Full slabs or half slabs are offered.

"My wife and I drive from Northern Kentucky to eat their ribs," said one customer. "They're as good as it gets."

108

This is one barbeque joint that lets you do it your way when it comes to preparing your pork or brisket with sauce. Each table has five bottles, with a different sauce. First there's the Memphis Sweet, then the Texas Spicy, and the Carolina Mustard, the North Carolina Spicy Vinegar, and finally the Kentucky Small Batch. You don't see this at most places.

You may not think a barbeque joint would have a sophisticated dessert, but this one does. They've taken some good old Valentine vanilla ice cream that's made in Winchester, Kentucky, crushed bourbon balls into it and spread it on top of peach bread pudding. You've got to figure out a way to save room for this!

DINERS INFORMATION

Address:
4020 Georgetown Road
Hours:
Sunday-Wednesday, 11 a.m. – 10 p.m.
Thursday-Saturday, 11 a.m. – 11 p.m.
Phone:
859-233-7898
Price Range: $$
Area Attractions:
Kentucky Horse Park, Toyota Plant

Ricardo's Grill & Pub

VERSAILLES, KENTUCKY

This restaurant is located inside an old depot, and not only does it look good on the outside, it looks even better inside. This, along with a big city menu, has quickly turned owner Rick Radar's eatery into a destination spot to dine.

"We wanted to make this a special place," Rick says.

And he has.

General manager Josh Westfall has put together offerings you don't find just anywhere, and it all starts with appetizers that could easily qualify as meals, if not shared by two or three customers. There's a lot to choose from, including grouper fingers, banana peppers, smoked salmon, but the show stopper is the fried green tomatoes. There's a really good chance you haven't seen fried green tomatoes presented like this.

"We get raves about this," Josh says. "It's got our aloha shrimp sauce on it."

The sauce, along with several shrimp is poured on top of the lightly battered tomatoes to make them unlike any you've tasted.

Entrees are varied as well. Crab cakes, New Orleans pasta, bacon wrapped pork medallions, shepherd's pie, Atlantic salmon, shrimp and grits, ribs, sirloin and ribeye offer something for any size appetite. By the way, you don't see it often, but the Kentucky hot brown is served in a half or full order.

An assortment of burgers, clubs, chicken and fish sandwiches are offered.

Ricardo's has a beautiful bar area, with plenty of tables that are in addition to a separate dining space. In warm weather eating on the outside deck is very popular.

DINERS INFORMATION

Address:
110 Frankfort Street
Hours:
Monday-Thursday, 11 a.m. – 10 p.m.
Friday-Saturday, 11 a.m. – 11 p.m.
Sunday, 11 a.m. – 10 p.m.
Phone:
859-873-3663
Price Range: $$
Area Attractions:
Keeneland Race Track, Woodford Reserve Distillery

Shack in the Back BBQ

FAIRDALE, KENTUCKY

Shack in the Back, just outside of Louisville, is mainly a barbeque restaurant, but for certain it's much more than brisket, pork and wings. They're good all right, but so are the smoky turkey ribs, smoked chicken salad, and, yes the smoked meat loaf.

"I live in southern Indiana and drive over here every chance I get," said one customer.

"I work at Ford (Plant), and anytime we have out of town visitors we bring them here to eat," said another.

It's common for lunch visitors to order their "que" by the pound and split it at their table.

The parking lot here begins to fill up at 11 a.m. when the doors open.

Shack in the Back is an old 1896 log cabin that was once the home of Claude and Lennie Murphy (relatives of Hall of Fame Fairdale High School basketball coach Lloyd Gardner). Later, it became a florist shop and then in 2006 Mike and Barbara Sivells opened their long-time dream of a restaurant that served barbeque. The name came from an old garage they had once seen in the back of a house Mike was pressure washing years ago.

"We called it the "garage in the back," and as soon as we saw our old log cabin, we had the name," says Barbara.

The options here are plentiful and so are the various sauces. But the one that gets your attention is the white lightening sauce. It's not particularly

overpowering hot, but its combination of mayonnaise and vinegar makes for a tasty blend with just about anything you order.

"Lots of places in Kentucky offer burgoo," Mike says. "But we like to think ours is different. Our customers sure do like it."

A 50-seat addition was added to the 24 seats in the main cabin several years ago to help better serve the large Friday and Saturday crowds. On those nights, hickory grilled ribeyes are on the menu.

This is one of those places when you leave, even as content as you are, you'll start thinking about when you can come back.

Address:
406 Mt. Holly Road (just off Gene Snyder Parkway)
Hours:
Monday-Thursday, 11 a.m. — 8 p.m.
Friday-Saturday, 11 a.m. — 9 p.m.
Closed Sunday
Phone:
502-363-3227
Price Range: $
Area Attractions:
Jefferson Memorial Forest

Stinky and Coco's

WINCHESTER, KENTUCKY

Some people say it's all about the view, but at Stinky and Coco's it's more than just the view ... it's also about the food. This very well may become your favorite restaurant, and when you order the shrimp and grits, it just might become your favorite meal.

Don Parsons has had his restaurant in Winchester since 2009 with a mission of bringing this scenic town some comfort food with a real southern flair.

Stinky and Coco's is located with a scenic view of a public golf course, with 60 inside seats and another 32 on the beautiful patio.

Stinky and Coco's is named after Don's two cats, so he must really love them.

You'll love the po'boys, melts and burgers, as well as the Chorizo eggs, a combination of sausage, potatoes, green onions, and salsa and queso fresco in scrambled eggs.

Meatloaf is a Friday special. It's already a Winchester classic, prepared with ground sugar, bell peppers, milk, crackers and onions with a ginger glaze and a hint of ketchup.

"We offer some really good dinner specials at night," Don says. "Among them are the blackened catfish, rockfish, steaks, dry rubbed ribs, grilled chicken and pork chops."

A full service bar is available.

Winchester and Clark County are known as the Beer

Cheese Capital of Kentucky, even to the point of a Blue Cheese Trail, and Stinky and Coco's is a part of it. That's why the beer cheese fries just might be an I-must-order-item.

DINERS INFORMATION

Address:
175 Clubhouse Drive
Hours:
Tuesday-Saturday, 8 a.m. – 8:30 p.m.
Sunday-Monday, 8 a.m. – 2:30 p.m.
(Winter hours subject to change)
Phone:
859-745-1800
Price Range: $$
Area Attractions:
Beer Cheese Trails and Festival, Lower Howard's Creek Nature Preserve, Fort Boonesborough, Kentucky River, Ale-8-One Tour; Civil War Driving Tour, Downtown Walking Tour.

Stull's Country Store

"We're officially in Payneville," says owner Marlinda Stull, whose parents bought the old store back in 1972. "It was Andyville until the post office closed."

Stull's really is a country store. It offers groceries, staples, a full deli, and there's even a gas pump that sits right outside the front door.

"I like to tell everybody that comes by that if we don't have it you probably don't need it," says Marlinda who goes by the name of Mauri. "I'm not trying to compete with Walmart or Kroger, but I tell my customers I'll take care of them and my prices are competitive."

Stull's Country Store, however, is all about their food, especially during the summer months when a giant smoker sitting outside seems to be going 24/7.

"We've got smoked Cajun turkey, hams, bologna, brisket, pulled pork and ribs," Mauri adds. "With our dinners we serve your choice of baked beans, potato salad, pasta salad or coleslaw."

Of course, you can also have an old-fashioned cheese and crackers if you want.

Every Friday in the fall, Stull's features pork tenderloin sandwiches and chili every day.

With the store's location being only a short distance from the Ohio River, Mauri says they get quite a bit of "river traffic" customers.

Several tables and chairs sit near the rear of the store for those who want to "sit a spell." And to further add to the ambiance a collection of antique toy pedal cars and old metal signs line the walls near the ceiling.

Address:
4385 Rhodelia Road
Hours:
Monday-Friday, 7 a.m. – 7 p.m. (Summer)
Saturday, 8 a.m. – 7 p.m.
Sunday, 9 a.m. – 3 p.m.
Monday-Sunday, 7 a.m. – 6:30 p.m. (Fall)
Phone:
270-496-4169
Price Range: $
Area Attractions:
Ohio River; Otter Creek Park

A.P. Suggins Bar & Grill

LEXINGTON, KENTUCKY

This is one of those restaurants that seems more like a neighborhood spot where all of the locals eat. For sure, the locals do indeed eat here, but so do lots of others in Lexington.

"Our location is one of the reasons for our success," says co-owner, David Lowe Ravencraft, who along with Jackson McReynolds and Brad Scott runs one of the most popular restaurants in Lexington.

When you walk through the front door, one side is the bar area with several high top tables. This side is where the action seems to be, with televisions, and lots and lots of chatter. On the other side the dining is a bit more subdued. But on either side the same good food can be ordered, and on either side you have a good chance of seeing current and former University of Kentucky coaches as well as past sports stars.

Suggins' is not all that far from the U of K campus, so it's rather handy during sporting events.

The menu is loaded with appetizers of a chili bowl, cheese fries, banana peppers, nachos and beer cheese plate. There's a list of sandwiches, of which there are too many to mention here. However, one should be talked about. It's the 1000 Island grilled turkey. Oh yes! Fresh turkey, Swiss cheese, and homemade 1000 Island on grilled wheat bread.

"All of the dressings are made fresh right here," David says.

Chicken finger salads, hot browns, chops, open faced turkey and roast beef are hits, too. But one of the most popular items is their Suggins' Special. It's a prime New York strip, seasoned and then grilled.

A.P. Suggins' is a high energy restaurant, especially at night. The wait staff is equal to the task with friendliness and efficiency. On weekends be prepared for a short wait.

DINERS INFORMATION ?

Address:
345 Romany Road
Hours:
Monday-Saturday, 11 a.m. – 10 p.m.
Closed Sunday
Phone:
859-268-0709
Price Range: $$
Area Attractions:
University of Kentucky, Rupp Arena, Keeneland Race Track, Kentucky Horse Park, Red Mile Race Track, Talbott Todd

Wagner's Pharmacy

LOUISVILLE, KENTUCKY

S ome say this drug store-restaurant has just about as much history as nearby Churchill Downs.

Open since the 1920's, this is one place horse owners, stall cleaners, jockeys, and hot walkers can rub elbows while enjoying a good breakfast of ham and eggs, or a hot sandwich and cherry coke for lunch.

For race fans, it's a great place to visit and take in all of the store's history, and maybe even get a hot tip to go along with your cup of coffee.

There's an actual pharmacy and tack room in the back, but up front, where the lunch counter and comfortable booths are, is where all of the action is.

The walls, and even the building's support columns, are covered with old pictures of horses and the horsemen who walked, trained and rode them. The pictures, much like the customers, are of both the famous and not so famous.

Wagner's is not really one of those early bird places that open before dawn. Instead, it opens at 8 a.m. That's when much of the early, early morning chores are out of the way across the street and the horse people can sit down to a serious breakfast.

SINCE 1922   WAGNER'S   SINCE 1922

Lunch is also big. Soups, sandwiches, meatloaf and shakes are just a sampling.

As one might expect, this is a place that caters to horse people. But it also caters to people who enjoy good food in a southern style setting.

Wagner's is a great place to pick up a Derby souvenir, tip sheet, and Daily Racing Form.

Lee Wagner, the store's owner, died a few years ago after putting a lifetime into making this a wonderful place to not only eat, but to visit. Today, son Lee, daughters Brenda and Karen carry on with the business.

DINERS INFORMATION

Address:
3113 S. Fourth Street
Hours:
Monday-Friday, 8 a.m. – 3 p.m.
Saturday & Sunday when Churchill is open, 8 a.m. – 3 p.m.
Phone:
502-375-3800
Price Range: $
Area Attractions:
Churchill Downs, Kentucky Derby Museum

Annie Ruby's Café	Burkesville, KY
Ariella Bistro & Bar	Russellville, KY
Bethel Dipper	Russellville, KY
Boyce General Store	Alvaton, KY
Chaney's Dairy Barn	Bowling Green, KY
City Pool Hall	Monticello, KY
Coe's Restaurant	Russell Springs, KY
Fishtales	Nancy, KY
Freedom Store & Restaurant	Freedom, KY
Frosty Freeze	Franklin, KY
Gone Fishin'	Morgantown, KY
Guthrie's River House	Burnside, KY
Hardscratch Country Store	Columbia, KY
Hickory Hill BBQ	Scottsville, KY
Lake Cumberland State Resort Park	Jamestown, KY
Micqueal's Bistro	Glasgow, KY
Paradise Point	Scottsville, KY
Tea Bayou	Bowling Green, KY

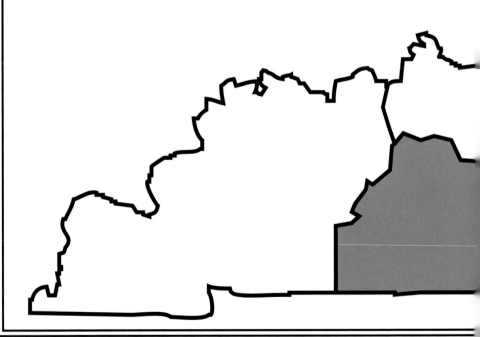

SOUTH CENTRAL
REGION

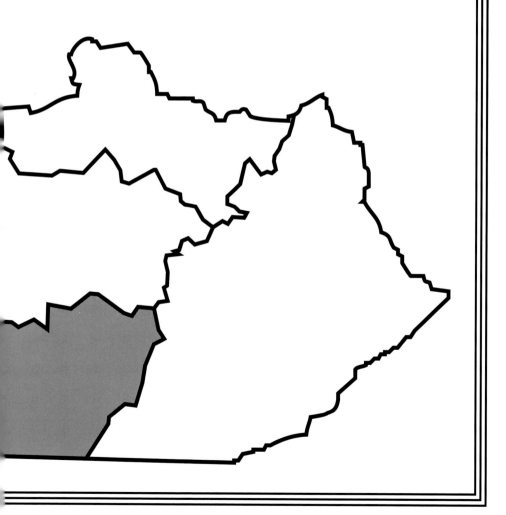

Annie Ruby's Café

BURKESVILLE, KENTUCKY

It's somewhat unexpected. But right in the center of downtown Burkesville on Courthouse Square is Annie Ruby's Café.

In the same space that was occupied by Smith Pharmacy, a business that dates back to 1908, Heather and David Hannan decided to open a restaurant a few years ago. And did they ever!

Annie Ruby's is a breakfast and lunch eatery only, and it has become so popular with the locals you'll need to get there early or you'll probably wait for a seat. If you do, you can look around at this old drugstore furnishings that date back to the early 1900's.

Heather and David decided their place wouldn't be just another spot to eat, instead it would be one that serves up delicious, and at the same time, healthy meals.

"We don't do burgers and fries," says Heather. "We do everything fresh daily, and what we don't grow ourselves, we buy locally."

They grow their own lettuce, peppers, cucumbers, corn, potatoes, and tomatoes. And the pickles they serve? They make them, too.

Their Heirloom Tomato Pie is one of their best selling items. So, too, is the grilled cheese Panini, pimento cheese salad, and the chicken salad. And when you think you are all finished, well, there's the butterscotch pie. You heard right!

Heather grew up in Burkesville and with husband David, spent 13 years in the Cayman Islands where she was an interior designer and he worked in real estate. Burkesville, and anyone who eats at Annie Ruby's, sure is glad they are back home.

DINERS INFORMATION

Address:
204 Courthouse Square
Hours:
Monday-Friday, 7 a.m. – 10 a.m. (Breakfast)
Monday-Friday, 11 a.m. – 2 p.m. (Lunch)
Phone:
270-864-2664
Price Range: $
Areas of Interest:
Dale Hollow State Resort

Ariella Bistro & Bar

RUSSELLVILLE, KENTUCKY

"You'll have to go to Baltimore to get a crab cake as good as mine," says Deborah Hirsch, chef-owner of Ariella.

But no one has to travel that far east. All you have to do is make it to downtown Russellville, where you'll find a big city restaurant in a beautiful small town.

Deborah brings an excitement for not only good food, but for the total dining experience for her customers.

"We want our restaurant to look great and the food even greater," she says.

Deborah likes to jokingly tell people she got to Russellville by making two wrong turns. But the truth is, she and her husband, Richard, wanted to get away from Atlantic City, New Jersey and find a southern home. When you eat at Ariella, you'll be glad they chose Kentucky and especially Russellville.

The Hirschs' bought an old downtown building that in its day served as a print shop. They took it down to the bare walls and from there created this fantastic eatery that seats 65 on the main floor and another 85 upstairs for special occasions.

Each booth has a high back that creates a bit more privacy when it comes to conversation.

"We cook authentic Italian with a touch of American flavor," says Deborah, who adds that the seafood here is flown in weekly. "I

had some uncles who had restaurants in Baltimore, so believe me I know good seafood."

Pasta dishes here are described as old world, meaning they are really good. Lasagna, baked cheese ravioli, clams linguine, and chicken fettuccini Alfredo are just a few of the too-many-to-list offerings.

Thursday, Friday and Saturday only, Deborah prepares her "fresh catch" seasonal with the fish being flown in within 24 hours of the catch. As you might expect after reading this, salmon, scallops, pork tenderloin and steaks are also served.

"We want to have something for everyone that walks through our door, so we serve a wonderful assortment of burgers as well as specialty pizzas," Deborah adds.

It may surprise some that Russellville now has a destination restaurant .… but it does, indeed.

DINERS INFORMATION

Address:
183 S. Main Street
Hours:
Tuesday-Friday, 11 a.m. – til crowd leaves
Saturday, 5 p.m. – til the crowd leaves
Closed Sunday and Monday
Phone:
270-731-0004
Price Range: $$$
Area things of interest:
Historic home walking tour, Tobacco Festival, Bank robbed by Jesse James

Bethel Dipper

RUSSELLVILLE, KENTUCKY

The Bethel Dipper is a place where everybody may not know your name, but by most accounts they know what the locals are going to order.

Since 1953, this two-window walk-up restaurant has been dishing out soft-serve ice cream, shakes, malts, sundaes, sandwiches, chilidogs, cheeseburgers, grilled cheese, sloppy Joes and onion rings.

Back in the old days Bethel College was in Russellville, but many of the entities around town still incorporate the name, and that's what owner Nancy Powell's grandfather did when he started the business.

Nancy had graduated from the University of Kentucky, with plans to become a teacher when she decided to help her father out at the Dipper.

"I soon found out I wanted to carry on the tradition here," she said. "It was a good business and I liked it."

Don't be in a real hurry here. It's one of those order-and-wait-in-your-car places, and from the time they open at 9 a.m. 'til closing, there is a constant line of customers.

"I live in Bowling Green, 26 miles away, but whenever I'm here I come here," said one customer. "I always order the same thing every time … cheeseburger, fries and a shake."

Nancy Powell says their customers are so

consistent that "as soon as we see 'em pull up in the parking lot we know what they want."

The Bethel Dipper is one of those days-gone-bye restaurants that has managed not to get left behind.

DINERS INFORMATION

Address:
200 S. Bethel Street
Hours:
Monday-Saturday, 9 a.m. – 9 p.m.
Sunday, 10 a.m. – 8 p.m.
Phone:
270-726-7571
Price Range: $
Area Attractions:
Shaker Museum, stately home walking tour, James Gang Bank Robbery

Boyce General Store

ALVATON, KENTUCKY

This general store has been serving customers in one form or another since 1869, but it has been only the last few years that it has been cranking out food that customers have been traveling from near and yonder to eat.

Brie and Brad Golliher have taken a local landmark located 10 miles from Bowling Green and made it better. They have put their heart and soul into the food they turn out, and what in the beginning was just for the locals, now has car after car pulling into the parking lot with their out of county and out of state license plates.

From the time you walk up the front porch steps and pull open the two large screen doors, you realize this is how it used to be. The days are long gone since customers came by to get groceries and household staples they needed at home. Brie and Brad, however, have just enough of them lining the shelves to keep it interesting.

But it's the tables, chairs and the large grill at the rear of the store that screams, "Let's eat!"

Breakfast starts at 6 a.m. and is served til 10 a.m. It's all the usual, plus country ham, steak and tenderloin. However, it's the dinner that turns things up a notch at the Boyce General Store.

The nightly specials of fried chicken sandwiches, deli sandwiches, chuck wagons, tenderloins, Friday night catfish, hushpuppies, and hand cut fries that customers can't seem to get enough of.

130

"We're all about fresh," Brad says. "Ninety-percent of our food is locally sourced. We get our beef from Downing Cattle Co. in Fountain Run (located in a nearby county), and it's delivered to us fresh."

All of the chicken, catfish and tenderloins are hand breaded. And the slaw, tartar sauce, and hushpuppies are made from scratch.

A large covered patio with a bandstand sits just outside the back-side door, and on Friday and Saturday nights the place is really alive.

"Brie and I had no idea our business would evolve into what it has," says Brad. "We're just trying to keep up."

And keep up they have!!

Brie, who grew up not far from the old store, is called a "pieologist" for the delicious pies and cookies she bakes, so when you get there, go ahead and order your slice, because they go fast.

DINERS INFORMATION

Address:
10551 Woodburn Allen Springs Road (Hwy. 240)
Hours:
Monday-Thursday, 6 a.m. — 4:30 p.m.
Friday, 6 a.m. — 7:30 p.m.
Saturday, 6 a.m. — 3 p.m.
Closed Sunday
Phone:
270-842-1900
Price Range: $
Area Attractions:
National Corvette Museum; Lost River Cave, Historic L & N Railpark;
Beech Bend Park & Raceway; Aviation Heritage Park.

Chaney's Dairy Barn

BOWLING GREEN, KENTUCKY

Back in 2002 Carl Chaney and his wife Debra weren't quite sure what they were going to do with their dairy farm located on the outskirts of Bowling Green. The farm had been in the family since 1888, and operated as a dairy farm since 1940, so the family discussion was a serious matter.

The Chaney's had witnessed the downward spiral of milk prices, and realized if they were going to keep the farm they needed to come up with an answer. And after research and conversation with other farmers, they finally had the answer — ice cream!

They had done their homework, and today Chaney's Dairy Barn has become one of the most unique eating experiences in all of Kentucky.

You can't miss the big red replica of a dairy barn. It's one busy place.

Located on 31-W between Bowling Green and Franklin, Chaney's

not only offers their signature ice cream treats, but also homemade sandwiches, soups, pies and all kinds of specials.

"We never imagined it would get to this," says Carl Chaney. "But the best part of it all is that we were able to carry on the family farm.

The homemade soups (I recommend the potato), chicken salad, burgers, turkey sandwiches, grilled turkey and cheese, grilled ham and cheese, are all tasty. For something different try the Spicy Bird, a spicy fried chicken breast patty with lettuce, tomato, and pepper jack cheese, served with ranch or honey mustard on a toasted bun. Salads and kid-friendly menu are also available. Whatever you get also add their homemade ranch seasoned kettle chips.

Regardless of how full you are, I can promise you'll find room for the ice cream. It's what put Chaney's on the map and they sell some 20,000 gallons of it a year.

The eating area has expanded to now seat 100, and a Kentucky product gift shop compliments it all.

DINERS INFORMATION

Address:
9191 Nashville Road (31-W South)
Hours:
Monday-Saturday, 6 a.m. – 8 p.m.
Sunday, 12 noon – 5 p.m.
Summer hours extended
Phone:
270-843-5567
Price Range: $
Area Attractions:
Corvette Museum, Lost River Cave, Beech Bend Park and Raceway, Aviation Park, L & N Railway Museum

133

City Pool Hall

L ots of small towns across Kentucky had one of these type restaurants back in the day. A few still do, and Monticello is one of them.

It's like a ritual for anyone who ever lived in this Wayne County town and moved away, and then comes back. A stop at the City Pool Hall in the middle of downtown is a must.

Since 1946 when they first opened their doors, people far and near have been stopping by for a hamburger or two. Keep in mind this is a pool hall that serves hamburgers and hot dogs.

"We don't do fries," says Michael Samuels, one of the restaurants grill men. "We have bags of chips, though."

A counter with a handful of red-topped backless stools put customer's right smack in front of a grill full of patted burgers that are served on wax paper.

In the rear of the restaurant are four green felt covered pool tables, just as you would expect in a "city pool hall."

Former Olympian and Wayne County basketball great Kenny Davis doesn't miss a chance to stop in at the City Pool Hall when he returns

to his hometown to visit.

"You can't come back to Monticello without stopping in for a hamburger," Davis says. "Anyone who has ever lived in Wayne County knows about this place."

Over the years, the City Pool Hall was pretty much a "man only" establishment, like pool halls across the country. But now it is commonplace to see ladies sitting at the counter or waiting for their carryout order to be completed.

Yes, indeed, things are pretty basic at this burger joint, and owner Jimmy Ballou plans to keep it that way. Why would you change something that's worked for some 70 years?

DINERS INFORMATION

Address:
11 South Main
Hours:
Monday-Saturday, 6 a.m. – 8 p.m.
Closed Sunday
Phone:
606-348-5541
Price Range: $
Area Attractions:
Lake Cumberland, houseboat manufacturing

135

Coe's Restaurant

RUSSELL SPRINGS, KENTUCKY

Back in 1972, George Coe and wife Geneva opened this Russell Springs restaurant, and over the years Coe's has become one of the most popular dining places in the region.

Today, son Gerald is running the restaurant in the same tradition as his dad, and even though the sign on the window touts its catfish, it is far more than a fish place.

"Our fish is big here," says Gerald. "We cut it ourselves and hand bread it. We take the time to do it right."

Coe's serves between 500 and 800 pounds of catfish a week.

And now, about some other popular items...

Frog legs, baked tenderloin, ribeyes, roast beef Manhattan, chicken, hamburger steak, salmon croquettes and delicious Penn's country ham, are just some of the offerings. You might think you can't get excited about side items at Coe's, but there's one you can. The home fries are blended with onions and peppers, and some customers make a meal out of them.

"We have people who have been eating with us for 30-35 years from Ohio, Virginia and Tennessee," says Gerald. "And one time, Gov. Wallace Wilkinson

helicoptered in and ate with us. So have country music stars Marty Stewart and Hank Williams, Jr., and wrestler Hacksaw Jim Duggin."

But two of the stars are already there. Lisa Poff and Ella Schmidt have been serving customers for close to 25 years, which further adds to the consistency of Coe's.

Pies and cobblers are made fresh each day on an alternating basis. Peach cobbler, and butterscotch, coconut and chocolate pies all quickly sell out.

Coe's is a lunch and supper place that seats about 100. You may have to wait for a table, but it's worth it.

DINERS INFORMATION

Adress:
Key Village Shopping Center at the intersection of KY. Hwy. 80 &
    Lakeway Drive
Hours:
Tuesday-Saturday, 10:30 a.m. – 9 p.m.
Closed Monday and Sunday.
Phone:
270-866-9980
Price Range: $
Area Attractions:
Lake Cumberland

Fishtales

For openers, one word can describe Fishtales at Wolf Creek Marina on Lake Cumberland. Wow! First of all, the recently updated marina is nice, but when you add a sophisticated dining experience right on the water, you have a destination restaurant with a menu to back it up.

It's nice to arrive at Fishtales by boat if you have one, but you don't have to. Cars can get you there, too.

Fishtales provide visitors with a Tiki South Florida flavor and a gorgeous panoramic view of Lake Cumberland.

"We want to make our customers feel like they just boated up in the Keys," says general manager Nancy Harden.

With a Key West trained chef, this waterside restaurant has no problem turning out top shelf eats.

"We offer a menu here unlike anything else on the lake," Nancy adds. "And not only is it good, Fishtales is fun."

Seafood selections include shrimp and grits, tuna rolls; Keys shrimp penne served with grape tomatoes and capers in a garlic olive oil sauce;

Mahi, grilled, fried or parmesan encrusted; parmesan encrusted scallops; red snapper Oscar topped with crab meat, asparagus and hollandaise sauce; fried calamari; Ahi tuna; cod fish sandwiches; jerk shrimp club croissant; and fish tacos; and smoked sea salt encrusted ribeye.

Fishtales serves up an assortment of sandwiches and gourmet burgers. Also on the dock is a top-of-the line Ship Store with the absolute latest in fashions.

This is a seasonal restaurant open from April 1 through October 31. The outside (under the thatched roof) area seats approximately 100 with an inside area that can handle 25.

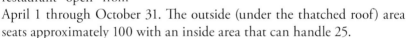

Fishtales might not be the easiest place to get to by car, but you can be assured it will be one of the most unusual in this book. At Nancy, Kentucky pick up Hwy. 3262 – 3 miles, dead-end highway 196 – 13 ½ miles to Hwy. 3277 – go straight. Boat tie-ups available.

DINERS INFORMATION

Address:
782 Island Ramp Road
Hours:
Monday-Sunday, 12 noon – 10 p.m.
April 1 – October 31
Phone:
270-866-3634
Price Range: $$
Area Attractions:
Lake Cumberland, State Park, Houseboat rentals

Freedom Store & Restaurant

FREEDOM, KENTUCKY

The address might say Glasgow, but believe me, it's not. Freedom Store is located halfway between Glasgow and Tompkinsville on Highway 63 in the itsy-bitsy community of Freedom.

"We're about 12 miles out of Glasgow," says owner Lee Ann Bragg, who along with husband Willard decided they wanted to do something different in life.

"This place has been a store for over 90 years, but we took it over back in 2008," Willard added.

It really is a general store. Shelves along the wall offer bread, cookies, grocery items, hardware, bailer twine, gloves, health care items, and a few nuts and bolts. But make no mistake about it, it is Lee Ann's food that brings 'em in.

The locals start arriving at 6 a.m. for breakfast each day, and then some of the same ones are back at lunch, and then if they're real hungry they may even be back before the store closes at 4 p.m. It's that good.

Freedom serves up an assortment of sandwiches that includes burgers, chicken, tenderloin, grilled cheese and bologna; ham and turkey as cold sandwiches, but it's those daily specials that really do it. Country fried steak, meatloaf, salmon patties, pork tenderloin, country ham casserole, and Salisbury steak are a few.

But here's a hint. If you can get to Freedom on Friday, it's skillet fried chicken day. Call ahead and ask, "What's cookin'?"

140

"We start cookin' it at 11 a.m., and sometime all we have is gone by noon," says Lee Ann.

The curly Q fries are a topic of conversation here. Willard bought a potato cutting apparatus at a yard sale sometime back and he proudly says an order of the specialty fries is made from one whole fresh potato.

Saturday is catfish day here … yes, with hushpuppies and a couple of sides.

DINERS INFORMATION

Address:
13200 Tompkinsville Road
Hours:
Monday-Friday, 6 a.m. – 4 p.m.
Saturday, 6 a.m. – 3 p.m.
Closed Sunday
Phone:
270-427-5025
Price Range: $
Area Attractions:
Lakes, Rollercoaster Highway Yard sale first weekend in October

141

Frosty Freeze

FRANKLIN, KENTUCKY

Years ago I-65 by-passed Franklin, and when it did it also by-passed the Frosty Freeze on the south end of town on 31-W. But, in spite of it, the town and the three-windowed walk-up restaurant have both thrived.

Willis and Mary Yokley opened their now-legendary Frosty Freeze in 1956, and all of these years later it's still much like it was.

"We've still got the original fountain and grill, says owner Wendy Gant, who started working there in 1975 as a teenager, and then with her husband Donny bought the restaurant in 2005. "The awning and sign out front are original, too."

From the time they open at 9 a.m. until they close at night the customers come in a steady stream. And license plates in the parking lot reveal as many from Tennessee as Kentucky.

"Our most popular items are the baby burgers, banana shakes, and cherry Coke," Wendy says. "And the cherry Cokes are made with syrup."

If you think a milk shake is just a shake, think again. The banana shake has so many chunks of banana; you really need a spoon instead of a straw.

As you might expect, ice cream eats and drinks are big. Hand-scooped ice cream and soft-served vanilla is the fare.

An assortment of sandwiches that

include homemade Sloppy Joes, tenderloin, chuckwagon, homemade pimento cheese, chilidogs, and fried pickles are all popular.

Be prepared for a short wait. The food here is fresh. They don't just hand it to you as soon as you order. In fact, they don't cook it until you order.

"One couple comes here so often when they get out of their car all they do is hold up two fingers," laughs Wendy. "That means they want two chuckwagons, two fries and two teas.

Several picnic tables and a couple of benches sit out front.

The Frosty Freeze back in the day was close to the edge of town, but now as Franklin has grown, it's close to being in the middle.

DINERS INFORMATION

Address:
433 S. Main, Hwy. 31-W
Hours:
Monday-Thursday, 9 a.m. – 10 p.m.
Friday-Saturday, 9 a.m. – 10:30 p.m.
Closed Sunday
Phone:
270-586-5365
Price Range: $
Area Attractions:
Kentucky Downs Race Track, Kenny Perry's Country Creek Golf Course

Gone Fishin'

MORGANTOWN, KENTUCKY

Gone Fishin' is one of the more unique restaurants in these pages for several reasons. One of which is its location a few miles outside of Morgantown and a mile or so from the William H. Natcher Parkway in Butler County.

The restaurant is inside of a big, blue metal building that was originally constructed for a farm-raised fish processing facility. It's easy to miss.

Teresa Lindsey and husband Bobby own and operate the restaurant that seats up to 130 customers.

Another thing that makes the place unique is they are open only two days a week ... Thursday and Friday!

"We open about 10:30 in the morning and close when they've stopped coming and we've fed them all," laughs Teresa.

It's a unique approach to accommodating the customer, but it's been working here since they opened in 2005.

This is definitely one restaurant that has flown under the publicity radar for sure. But one look at their menu and you might say, "What took me so long?"

How about frog legs, shrimp, snow crab, oysters, stuffed crab, tilapia, snapper, grouper, Mahi and catfish, all prepared and presented in various combinations.

Appetizers include gator bites, fried clams, peel and eat shrimp, hush puppies and crab rangoon.

One of the unique items is the Low Boil that includes shrimp, snow crab, smoked sausage, potatoes, onions and corn-on-the cob. It feeds about three people, depending on how hungry you are.

There's also Angus chopped steak and chicken tenders for those who may not want seafood.

"We have our seafood shipped in from Gulf Shores, Alabama," Teresa adds. "We want quality here, and we don't cook it 'til it's ordered."

The desserts aren't bad either. Can you say peanut butter pie? How about Key Lime or coconut cream?

DINERS INFORMATION

Address:
3300 Bowling Green Road (Hwy. 231)
Hours:
10:30 a.m. — til the customers stop coming
Thursday and Friday only
Phone:
270-526-8917
Price Range: $$
Area Attractions:
Green River Museum

Guthrie's River House

Don't say you weren't warned. This is a good place to eat with a good scenic view of Lake Cumberland.

In an odd sort of way, Guthrie's is located in Burnside but its official address is Somerset. There are lots of Kentucky towns that seem to have this confusion.

But what's not confusing is the food served here.

"We're a steakhouse," offers owner Angelique Guthrie. "We serve hand cut USDA meat, and we have people who come to the lake from all over the United States who eat here and tell us our steaks are the best they've ever eaten."

This location has been a restaurant since the 1960's, but several years ago Angelique and her husband William, both award winning chefs, took things over, and the sophistication they have added to basically simple food separates this restaurant from many of the others. For instance what might be a BLT someplace else is grilled salmon BLT here served on a Kaiser roll. Wow! And then there's the jalapeño Queso Burger, Angus beef with pickled jalapenos, lettuce, tomatoes, onion and topped with house queso sauce. The list of sandwiches goes on and on.

This restaurant's menu offers up seafood that runs a close second to the steaks.

"Our seafood here is fresh. That's why it's so good," says Angelique. "And we also make our own salad dressings."

Salmon, shrimp, crab stuffed tilapia, pan-seared Chilean sea bass, Mahi and catfish make up a delicious selection of seafood offerings.

"Our catfish is prepared from the original recipe back in about 1960 when this was known as Lakeview Restaurant," she said. "We've stayed true to the way it was first served here."

Dessert choices are plentiful, but have at least one person in your group to order the 7-layer white chocolate raspberry cake. It is white cake layered with butter cream frosting and raspberry filling.

As might be expected from a lake area restaurant the menu is subject to seasonal changes.

DINERS INFORMATION

Address:
6075 S. Highway 27
Hours:
Monday, 4 p.m. – 9 p.m.
Tuesday-Thursday, 11 a.m. – 9 p.m.
Friday-Saturday, 11 a.m. – 10 p.m.
Sunday, 11 a.m. – 8 p.m.
Phone:
606-802-2922
Price Range: $$
Area Attractions:
Lake Cumberland

Hardscratch Country Store

The post office at Hardscratch is long gone, but the Hardscratch Country Store, a few miles outside of Columbia, is still there and that's a good thing.

"I think the store was built in 1930," said one gentleman while he was sitting on a bench in front of the store catching up on the latest news.

Hardscratch is one of those community stores that still functions as a general store, but is primarily a place to eat some good country food. Two gas pumps sit out front, and inside owners Tim and Sherri Kelley have retained the original purpose of the business by offering up general purpose items customers and travelers on the way to Lake Cumberland might need.

"We're a shortcut to the lake here on 55," Tim Kelley says. "We try to offer up some things people might not normally get."

What he's talking about is a place that opens at 5 a.m., six days a week and 6 a.m. on Sunday. The 44-seat store turns out an assortment of breakfast choices that include eggs, sausage, and hash browns. Also available are rolls of bologna and Dixie loaf ready to be sliced and placed between two oversized saltine crackers.

Hardscratch serves a delicious, never frozen, half-pound burger that Tim says is his signature offering.

"Our burgers are different," Tim offers. "It's a special recipe that came

148

from the old Pool Room that used to be in Columbia."

This is more than a sandwich place. One Sunday a month fried chicken is served. There's also ham, roast beef Manhattan with mashed potatoes, slaw and fried apples. Oh yes, and there's the turkey and dressing, and all the trimmings.

The locals say the name Hardscratch is a symbol of faith, courage and hard work.

Now they can add good food.

DINERS INFORMATION

Address:
7694 Hwy. 55 South
Hours:
Monday-Saturday, 5 a.m. – 6 p.m.
Sunday, 6 a.m. – 2 p.m.
Phone:
270-384-4671
Price Range: $
Areas of Interest:
Lake Cumberland

Hickory Hill BBQ

SCOTTSVILLE, KENTUCKY

"It's the best barbeque anywhere around here," offered one customer as she walked to her car with a friend.

She was talking about Hickory Hill Barbeque, located in the roadside community of Hickory Hill three miles from Scottsville on Highway 100 in the Mennonite and Amish sections of Allen County.

Justin and Rebecca Howard now own and run the business that was first opened by friend Ron Keen in 2008.

Hickory Hill is a walk-up only eatery with four umbrella-picnic tables out front. A small very inviting covered front porch allows customers to step up to the window and order from an extensive menu featuring barbeque prepared over several open pits out back.

"Our atmosphere is all about backyard dining," says Rebecca, who grew up in the Paducah area, as did Justin. "We're proud of some of the sauces we've developed as well as some of our specialty items.

One of those is BBQ nachos, which blends pulled pork with nacho cheese sauce.

"We do an ultimate nacho that has a combination of the pulled pork on one end, cheese sauce and baked beans in the middle and pulled chicken on the other end."

Speaking of those baked beans ... wow! Baked with a slight sweetness and loaded with slivers

of pork, they are outstanding. And so, too, is the vinegar slaw (it may be the best I've had).

Hickory Hill Barbeque for such a little place serves up a giant product. The sliced shoulder is so tender it falls apart, and the fall-off-the-bone baby back ribs are a must have. And they can be ordered ¼ slab, ½ slab or full.

Many of the offerings here are served with hoecakes, a cornbread-type concoction, that works as a sandwich or base for their wonderful eats to be piled on top.

It's not on the menu as a regular item yet, but ask about their yet-to be-named baked potato special. "We split it open and pile pulled pork on it, a few jalapeno peppers, sour cream, nacho cheese sauce, one of our barbeque sauces and then a green onion for effect," Rebecca said.

There's a kids menu that includes hot dogs, grilled cheese and a chocolate sundae.

Address:
2791 Franklin Road (Hwy.100)
Hours:
Friday, Saturday and Monday, 10 a.m. – 6 p.m.
Sunday, 12 noon – 5 p.m. (somewhat seasonal depending on weather, call ahead during winter)
Phone:
270-622-0508
Price Range: $
Area Attractions:
Amish/Mennonite farm produce

Lake Cumberland State Resort Park

JAMESTOWN, KENTUCKY

It's not even open for debate that Kentucky's State Parks are the finest in the nation. And one of the best is Lake Cumberland State Resort Park with its 63 lodge rooms and 30 cottages.

And right in the middle of it all is Rowena Landing Restaurant, located in Lure Lodge. This is a year-round, three-meals-a-day facility with spectacular water views.

Of course, the restaurant caters to those overnighting here, but also to those on nearby houseboats, and also the residents in surrounding towns.

Kentucky's parks are widely known for their buffets, but here the resident chef is able to be creative in selections and the way they are presented.

Penn's country ham with red-eye gravy is a solid standard. So too, is the catfish. But the star of the show might just be the hot brown. The baked country ham, roasted turkey, smothered in cheese sauce, topped with tomato, bacon, and cheddar, is then oven-baked until piping hot. It's a Kentucky-must.

There's also something called "Kentucky Country Fare". It's what we call country food and is it good: Pinto beans, fried potatoes, corncakes and coleslaw served with sliced onions.

Sandwiches, a salad bar and buffet are daily staples here.

Here at Lake Cumberland State Park outdoor fireplaces and grills allow for more dining experiences to be staged outside later in the year.

The Park takes pride in buying locally when possible, and is a participant in the Kentucky Proud program when it comes to food.

From March thru October on the third Friday of each month a seafood buffet is served.

DINERS INFORMATION

Address:
5465 State Park Road
Hours:
Daily, 7 a.m. – 10:30 a.m. (Breakfast); 11:30 a.m. – 4 p.m. (Lunch);
    Sunday Lunch, 12 p.m. – 4 p.m.
November 1 – April 30, 5 p.m. – 8 p.m.
May 1 – October 31, 5 p.m. – 9 p.m.
Phone:
270-343-3111 ext. 405
Price Range: $
Area Attractions:
Lake, Houseboats, State Dock

Micqueal's Bistro

Micqueal's sits just off the square in downtown Glasgow, a couple of doors down from the old Plaza Theatre.

Owner-chef Michael Matthews has assembled a menu that serves customers breakfast and lunch six days a week.

"We try to offer up a healthy, fresh and different selection of items not offered everywhere else," Michael says.

And he has accomplished that with a sophisticated menu that begins with breakfast.

An assortment of three-egg omelets include the Mediterranean, portabella and spinach, and Mexican. Waffles, pancakes, biscuit and sausage gravy are also popular.

But it's those lunches that pop at Micqueal's.

Fried green beans, Hummus plate, fried dill pickles and soup specials are some of the appetizer choices.

Salads, salads and more salads are a pleasant theme from spinach, to Cobb to grilled fish to a BLT salad.

Michael has something for everyone, and his "entrees" are just as impressive. Quiche, stuffed Portabella, and a pineapple boat reveal the range of choices diners have. House-made Benedictine cucumber spread, topped with lettuce, and bacon is a warm-weather treat. Sandwiches, too, include turkey, clubs, pork loin, fish, Reuben, fried chicken, BLT and burgers round out the choices.

DINERS INFORMATION

Address:
131 E. Main Street
Hours:
Monday-Friday, 7 a.m. – 3 p.m.
Saturday, 7 a.m. – 2 p.m.
Closed Sunday
Phone:
270-629-6427
Price Range: $
Area Attractions:
Barren River Lake, museum

Paradise Point

You top the hill on 31-E between Scottsville and Glasgow and there it is … Paradise Point, for sure one of the most unique and fun places you'll ever grab a bite to eat.

In 2009, John and Sebrina Erskine took an old vacated building a couple of minutes from Barren River State Park and opened a funky junk and art store and sold Hebrew National hot dogs out of a wiener stand in the front.

Today, they still sell all that stuff, and the hot dogs, too, but Paradise Point has now turned into a destination place to eat breakfast on Friday, Saturday and Sunday from March til the end of October.

Once their doors unlock, the parking lot suddenly becomes crowded.

"The breakfast thing actually came about by accident," John says. "Being near the lake, people like to get out, some earlier than others. And some would come by in the morning. We just tried out some things for ourselves and then shared it with a few customers."

Once word began to spread they began to add to their menu. And today, what has been added has turned into a feed.

The hashbrown casserole reminds some of a church pot-

luck. The cheesy, gooey, buttery, crunchy hash browns have become their most popular item.

Close behind is the cowboy casserole … bell peppers, onions, mushrooms spread over a layer of Steenbergen sausage with cheddar and Monterey Jack cheese and then mixed with farm fresh eggs and you have, not only a delight cowboys will love, but also cowgirls.

And that's not all!

Biscuits and gravy, sausage grit casserole, cheese grit casserole, French toast casserole, quiches, and tomato pie only add to choices visitors have.

With the absolutely fun look John has created in his front parking lot, it is difficult for anyone to pass Paradise Point with at least pulling over. And when you pull over, you can't resist going inside. Then we all know what happens.

DINERS INFORMATION

Address:
10300 New Glasgow Road, 31-E
Hours:
Open March thru the end of October
Open Thanksgiving Day, 9 a.m. – til ?
Friday-Sunday, 8 a.m. – 5 p.m.
Phone:
270-622-7422
Price Range: $
Area Attractions:
Barren River Lake

Tea Bayou

BOWLING GREEN, KENTUCKY

The name of this café might seem simple and normal enough, but at Tea Bayou simple and normal doesn't exist.

A few years ago Theresa and Greg Shea brought their New Orleans influence to Bowling Green's beautiful Fountain Square in downtown, and opened a Crescent City styled eatery and tea bar. Remember, nothing is simple here, but the Shea's have made Louisiana food and tea work.

It starts with a wide selection of Po' Boys that include Muffaletta (ham, salami, mozza, olive salad and provo); Phileaux (roast beef, ham, mozza, and slaw); Cochon (pulled pork, ham, bacon and provo); Chicken Salad (with grapes, apples and tarragon dressing); and a Rouxben (corned beef, or turkey, swiss, kraut all on rye).

There are others, too, that include catfish or shrimp baskets. The Bourbon Street Bayou Burger is unique; its 1/3 lb. of beef and a touch of pork that blend together for a burger treat not found just anywhere. The bourbon glaze, cheddar and bacon all add to a great kick-back sandwich.

Soups, salads, fried shrimp and grits, and Andouille, red beans and rice, all are a part of what Greg has brought to Tea Bayou.

And about those teas.

"We have quite a collection of teas here," Theresa says. "Of course we have it here, for home use and ship all over."

Teas, hot or iced, specialty freezes, and lattes, smoothies, pro-

tein drinks and java infusions are all on the menu.

"Our tea makes us unique," adds Theresa. "Our customers can have a quality experience in a small restaurant atmosphere.

Weather permitting, dining is available on the sidewalk under a canvas canopy, just across the street from historic Fountain Square.

Tea Bayou makes their breads, slaw, chicken salad and desserts from scratch. But here's the tip of the day. Don't leave without an order of beignets, an old New

Orleans treat. Theresa and Greg have brought their own touch of this legendary dessert to Bowling Green. Take a bag of 'em with you. Also available are beer, wine and a selection of mixed drinks.

Address:
906 State Street
Hours:
Monday-Tuesday, 9 a.m. – 6 p.m.
Wednesday-Thursday, 9 a.m. – 8 p.m.
Friday-Saturday, 9 a.m. – 9 p.m.
Closed Sunday
Phone:
270-904-3889
Price Range: $
Area Attractions:
Fountain Square Park, Lost River Cave, Beech Bend Park, National Corvette Museum, Historic L & N Railpark, Southern Kentucky Performing Arts Center

159

Anchor Grill	Covington, KY
Chandler's Restaurant & Bar	Maysville, KY
Colonial Cottage Inn	Erlanger, KY
Jane's Saddlebag	Union, KY
Jewell's On Main	Warsaw, KY
Leono's	Cynthiana, KY
Little Town & Country Restaurant	Bedford, KY
Otto's	Covington, KY
Parc Café	Maysville, KY
Parkview Country Inn	Augusta, KY
Tousey House	Burlington, KY
Welch's Riverside Restaurant	Carrollton, KY

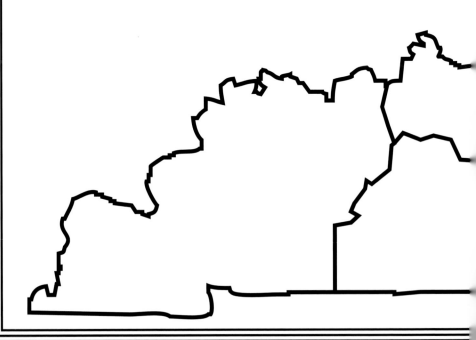

NORTHERN REGION

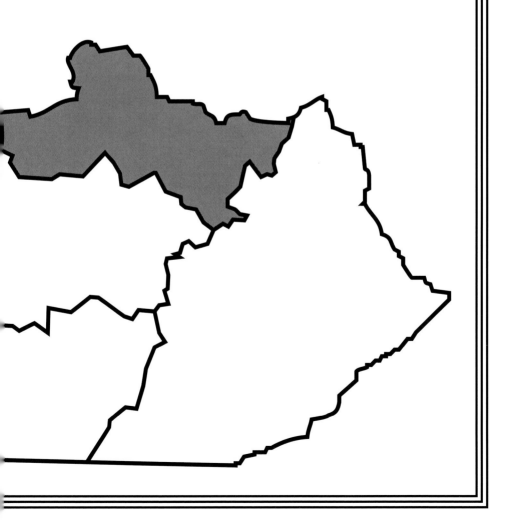

Anchor Grill

COVINGTON, KENTUCKY

You've got to get up early in the morning to get ahead of the Anchor Grill. You might as well forget it, because this is one of those 24/7 places that is legendary in northern Kentucky.

First opened in May 1946 by the Chapman family, Carolyn Chapman carries on the tradition in fine fashion. Their slogan is "We may doze, but we never close." But the truth is, they do in fact close on Christmas Day.

"That's the only day," Carolyn says. "But we usually have someone in here eating, even if it's family."

Breakfast is cooked to order, and as one would expect in an all-nighter customers can get just about anything, including a northern Kentucky specialty, goetta.

Sandwich platters and lots of "double deckers" are popular here.

The Anchor Grill offers a special menu between the hours of 10:30 a.m. to 9 p.m. It includes a 10 oz. strip steak, fried chicken, fried oysters, shrimp, roast beef and dressing, pork chops, liver & onions, and chicken and turkey wraps. A list of sides that include mashed potatoes, macaroni salad, carrots, hot slaw, fried zucchini and fried green tomatoes are served.

162

Missy Robinson, the manager, has been at the Anchor Grill for some 20 years, and it's easy to see why the customers like her.

"We serve our sweet potato casserole every Wednesday and Sunday," says Carolyn. "It's one of our best sellers."

For desserts, how about the carrot roll, peanut butter pie or cheesecake? They have all kinds of pies and cakes and ice cream.

You can't miss the huge painting on the side of the building. It's a photo op!

DINERS INFORMATION

Address:
438 Pike Street
Open:
24 hours – 7 days a week
Closed Christmas Day
Phone:
859-431-9498
Price Range: $
Area Attractions:
Newport Aquarium

Chandler's Restaurant & Bar

Maysville sits smack-dab on the Ohio River, and if you've ever been there you know it is one of the most charming places to visit in all of Kentucky.

Just like Mason County with all of its riverboat stories, many of the businesses here also have stories to tell.

One of those stories is Chandler's Restaurant and its owner Chan Warner.

Away from his regular job a few years ago, Chan used to barbeque out of his garage on weekends.

"Everybody seemed to like what I cooked, so I kept talking about opening a restaurant one day," he laughed.

Sure enough he did in 1994, and today he has turned all of that talk into one of the best restaurants in Maysville.

His 100-seat eatery is in a beautiful old building downtown, and as impressive as the outside is, the interior doesn't disappoint either.

Chandler's has a lunch menu and a dinner menu, with a beautiful bar right next door for those who want to wait there for a table or just to have a drink.

The lunch menu has an assortment of appetizers and salads, as well as a list of sandwiches that there's not enough room to mention all of them.

The dinner menu includes hand cut steaks (sirloin, fillet, angus, rib-eye), chicken livers, fried country ham, Porterhouse chops, hot browns, Bluegill filets, catfish, halibut, oysters, salmon, shrimp & grits, tilapia, and pasta. One of the pasta dishes that is really special is the artichoke pasta with shrimp and scallops prepared with a white wine garlic sauce.

Adult beverages of beer, wine and cocktails are available.

DINERS INFORMATION

Address:
212 Market Street
Hours:
Tuesday-Thursday, 11 a.m. – 9 p.m.
Friday-Saturday, 11 a.m. – 10 p.m.
Closed Sunday and Monday
Phone:
606-564-6385
Price Range: $$
Area Attractions:
Ohio River, flood wall murals, history museum

Colonial Cottage Inn

ERLANGER, KENTUCKY

Since 1933, this restaurant has been serving up some of the best food in northern Kentucky, and all of these years later, owners Matt and Noelle Grimes are carrying on the tradition.

"My family and I want to continue what was started decades ago by providing good food at good prices," Matt says.

The day at Colonial Cottage begins with breakfast, and as you might guess, they blow it out with all of the classics, from steak and eggs to omelets and casseroles to pancakes and waffles.

"One of our most popular dishes is goetta," Matt offers. "It's a regional food that is really big in this part of Kentucky."

Matt describes goetta as a combination of beef, pork, peppers, onions, and pin oats that's all cooked for six hours.

Sandwiches, burgers, prime rib, tuna melt and chicken combos are just a few of the offerings. Soups and salads partner up nicely with the country ham, New York strips, catfish and shrimp dinners. However, when you visit here make sure someone in your group orders the pan fried chicken.

"We've been recognized with the best fried chicken in northern Kentucky three years in a row," Matt adds.

This 140-seat restaurant serves its breakfast all day and there's a good chance one of the servers will be Linda Exler who has been delivering food to tables at the Colonial Inn for over 30 years.

Daily specials that change up regularly are the norm here, as is the Sunday brunch.

Last, but not least, are the desserts, of which the best known are the made from scratch cream pies. You will not believe the meringue. For sure, take a picture before the first bite.

DINERS INFORMATION

Address:
3140 Dixie Highway
Hours:
Monday-Saturday, 6:30 a.m. – 9 p.m.
Sunday, 7 a.m. – 9 p.m.
Phone:
859-341-4498
Price Range: $
Area Attractions:
Newport Aquarium, pro sports

Jane's Saddlebag

UNION, KENTUCKY

In 2004, Jane's Saddlebag was created. Peter's mother, Jane Blackmore, left an inheritance that was used to refurbish an old pioneer saddlebag home and turn this 35-acre property into something that families could visit and have fun.

Today, Jane's grandson Brett, wife Samantha, and good friend Tony DeMatteo have created a destination aptly named Jane's Saddlebag.

Located near Big Bone Lick State Park, and a few miles from Union in Boone County, this venue is packed full of history, creativity fun and yes, good food.

What they call the "main building" is where people gather to eat … inside or out.

"A couple of years ago, our burgers were named among the best in all of northern Kentucky," Brett says. "But we have other things, too."

But, first things first. The popular Woolly Mammoth Burger is 100% fresh sirloin, so no need to worry about anything prehistoric here.

Brats, hot dogs, grilled cheese, fruit plates, homemade mac & cheese, and Friday nights "steak night" are all very popular.

There are also a couple of dessert offerings: The Triple Layered Cheesecake topped with bourbon sauce, and the Frozen Ice Age Pie that is an ice cream pie made with homemade brownies and available in Cappuccino or peanut butter flavor. Beer and wine are also served.

Now, after you've eaten, you're ready to see what else there is to do here. And there is plenty.

A general store, wine shop, kids playland, petting zoo, kids village, hayrides, and a natural amphitheater with a replica of a 1700 flat boat, make this a place the entire family can enjoy.

"We're a heritage tourism destination," says Brett of his place on Big Bone Creek, a backwater of the Ohio River.

Jane's Saddlebag is seasonal, open from the beginning of April through October.

DINERS INFORMATION

Address:
13989 Ryle Road
Hours:
Friday, 11 a.m. – 8 p.m.
Saturday-Sunday, 11 a.m. – 7 p.m.
Phone:
859-991-3144
Price Range: $
Area Attractions:
Big Bone Lick State Park

Jewell's On Main

WARSAW, KENTUCKY

How many times have you heard the phrase "it's a hidden jewel?" Well, for sure there is a jewel on Main in downtown Warsaw, and it is in the form of one outstanding restaurant.

Rena and Justin Mylor have extensive experience in the food and hospitality business, and when the opportunity came about for them to return to their hometown and open a restaurant, they were all in.

"Our family was really behind us," says Justin. "It took a lot of work, with the help of my mom and dad in restoring the inside. It took us seven months."

An ankle injury to Justin slowed things down for several months, but when they did open they opened in grand style with a destination restaurant for this area.

Justin is a trained chef who likes to create as well as taking simple food products and turning them into "to die for eats."

"I cook with lots of bourbon," he says as he describes a bourbon peppercorn sauce he spoons over beef medallions

Jewell's On Main hand cuts their steaks, and hand slices their breaded fried green tomatoes.

Steaks, pork, chicken, fish, and pasta are staples at this wonderful restaurant. But

also, don't overlook the meatloaf and shrimp and grits. It's all good.

The salads are fresh and the soups are homemade, and with this said, folks around Warsaw sure are glad Rena and Justin decided to leave the corporate world and come home.

DINERS INFORMATION

Address:
100 E. Main Street
Hours:
Tuesday-Thursday, 11 a.m. – 9 p.m.
Friday, 11 a.m. – 10 p.m.
Saturday, 12 noon. – 10 p.m.
Closed Sunday and Monday
Phone:
859-567-1793
Price Range: $$
Area Attractions:
Kentucky Speedway, Ohio River

Leono's

CYNTHIANA, KENTUCKY

At Leono's, simple is better, and by this it refers to the outside and the menu on the inside. Nothing fancy-schmancy mind you, but for sure the food is really good.

Pizza might be the lead paragraph at Mary Beth Thomas' restaurant, but the rest of the story is all about her tasty pasta dishes.

From lasagna to fettuccini to spaghetti, pick your favorite and you will not be disappointed. The spaghetti can even be turned up a notch here with what Mary Beth calls Superghetti ... a combo of onions, mushrooms, green peppers, ham, peperoni, and meaty tomato sauce, topped with mozzarella.

Mary Beth has been on the food scene since 1988, and is quick, to say, "We start fresh every day with our pizzas. Nothing is carried over."

Leono's also serves up a selection of sandwiches that include Stromboli, beef and cheddar, hot ham & cheese (melted mozzarella, lettuce & tomato topped with a special dressing).

"Our turkey marinade salad and taco salad are big sellers here, too," says Mary Beth.

172

Lots of out-of-towners find their way to this Harrison County town just to eat at Leono's.

"We draw from northern Kentucky and all of the surrounding counties," she adds.

Leono's seats about 88 inside, and another 24 on the patio when weather permits.

DINERS INFORMATION

Address:
253 S. Church Street
Hours:
Monday-Thursday, 11 a.m. – 10 p.m.
Friday-Saturday, 11 a.m. – 11 p.m.
Sunday, 11:30 a.m. – 10 p.m.
Phone:
859-234-2517
Price Range: $
Area Attractions:
Harrison County Museum; writer Mark Mattmiller

173

Little Town & Country Restaurant

To say that Little Town & Country owner Bill Hughes is anything but a host would be an understatement.

Bill, who goes by the nickname of Big Eye from his legendary Corbin High School football days, bought the restaurant two years after it first opened, along with his brother, in 1959.

The walls of this restaurant look like a who's who gallery from his Corbin days and more recently pictures of U.S. Presidents and senators, and Kentucky governors who have stopped by to visit not only the crowd in this little restaurant, but also Big Eye.

One famous visitor didn't actually come inside, but instead stayed in his car and placed his order.

"They came and told me Elvis was outside," Bill laughed. "Heck, I went out there, introduced myself and shook his hand."

There's no menu here. You step to the front and order from the large board behind the counter.

"I've got some good food here and great employees," Bill proclaims. "One has been here for about 29 years, and then I've got a couple who are fairly new. They've only been with me 16 and 17 years."

Philly steak, patty melt, BLT with bologna, and double cheeseburgers are all popular. And at dinnertime country ham, chicken tenderloin, pork tenderloin, catfish and shrimp are in demand.

"We're proud of our desserts," says Bill. "Cream, fruit, and pecan pies are good, and so are our shakes and sundaes."

It's easy to see that Bill "Big Eye" Hughes likes to have fun. He is known to say in a joking way when he

sees friends, "check your gun at the door." Well, sometime back he said that, joking, of course, and the guy reached in his pocket and handed him his gun.

"I think he was a friend of mine from Corbin," laughed Bill.

DINERS INFORMATION

Address:
355 Highway 42 East
Hours:
Monday-Wednesday and Saturday, 7 a.m. – 8 p.m.
Thursday-Friday, 7 a.m. – 9 p.m.
Sunday, 8 a.m. – 2:30 p.m.
Phone:
502-255-3582
Price Range: $
Area Attractions:
Ohio River, Kentucky Speedway

Otto's
COVINGTON, KENTUCKY

Otto's is located in the heart of Mainstrasse in downtown Covington. This classy little restaurant opened in 2003, and seats approximately 50 including several comfortable stools at the bar.

Chef-Owner Paul Weckman seems to know his way around the kitchen, and it's never more evident than his menu offerings. There are two menus here: one for lunch and one for dinner.

This is a busy place with an atmosphere of customer chatter and unique dining choices. It's a fun and interesting restaurant with very good food that is not your run-of-the-mill.

Prosciutto and brie flatbread with figs and honeyed arugula is one of the choices as an appetizer. So are the fried green tomatoes and sweet potato fries.

Soups and salads are popular choices during lunchtime. Tomato dill soup, Otto's cobb salad, brie berry salad, sesame chicken, and kale and grain salads further show this is not an average dining spot.

Hot browns, tomato pie, seared salmon, pasta du jour along with a wide selection of cold sandwiches to include turkey cranberry, curry

chicken salad wrap, roast beef, and Otto's club are served.

"We're proud of all of our dishes," says Weckman. "We strive to serve quality food with first class service here, and continually make every effort to be the best."

Cuban sandwiches, along with the fresh veggie ciabatta (grilled veggie served on ciabatta with fresh mozzarella and homemade pesto), tilapia, and muffleotto further show the variety for lunch here.

Dinners here include beef tenderloin, shrimp and grits, sea scallops, bourbon marinated pork, seared salmon, braised short ribs and tuna nicoise.

DINERS INFORMATION

Address:
521 Main Street
Hours:
Monday-Friday, Lunch, 11:30 a.m. – 2:30 p.m.
Tuesday-Saturday, 5 p.m. – 10 p.m. (Dinner)
Sunday, 5 p.m. – 9 p.m.
Saturday-Sunday, 10 a.m. – 2 p.m. (Brunch)
Closed Monday evening
Phone:
859-491-6678
Price Range: $$
Area Attractions:
Mainstrasse, museums, professional sports in Cincinnati

Parc Café

MAYSVILLE, KENTUCKY

You might think you are in Paris, France, if you stroll down the sidewalk on 2nd Street in Maysville and come upon Parc Café.

"We definitely have a Parisian influence," says chef-owner Barb Goldman.

It begins with the outside cobblestone patio dotted with umbrella tables, and spills over to the interior of the café where huge windows allow lots of light to swarm over the marble flooring. The open airiness blends nicely with the dark wood that makes for a classy, yet very casual feel.

"Our menu is on the chalkboard and it changes daily," says Barb, who creates her often unique specials from what she buys locally.

Customers place their orders from the attractive counter, and can wait at one of the several tables or a big leather couch.

One of the soups is the Roast Autumn Vegetable with aged Gouda and topped with asiago cheese and bacon. Then there's quiche … you've got to try it.

The ham and biscuit here is not your typical biscuit. How about country ham with a bourbon mustard, apple butter sauce, Swiss and arugula all

on a homemade biscuit that was Barb's grandmother's recipe?

Other favorites are the open faced chicken pot pie, and the unbelievably delicious desserts.

"Our transparent pie is really good," says Barb. "It's simply eggs, sugar and cream."

And if that's not enough for your sweet tooth, perhaps the chocolate brownie with coconut infused bourbon or the bourbon bread pudding with chocolate, cinnamon and powdered sugar cooked in custard sauce and topped with bourbon caramel sauce. Can you say bourbon?

The Parc Café could be at home in any city, but Maysville residents are the lucky ones.

DINERS INFORMATION

Address:
35 E. 2nd Street
Hours:
Monday-Friday, 7:30 a.m. – 4 p.m.
Saturday, 8 a.m. – 4 p.m.
Closed Sunday
Phone:
606-564-9704
Price Range: $$
Area Attractions:
Flood wall murals, museum, shops

Parkview Country Inn

The village of Augusta was settled in 1795 on the Ohio River, and a few years later the original structure of the Parkview Country Inn was built and today it is on the state's historic register.

Not only is this a wonderful place to eat, but ten spacious guest rooms are available for overnight lodging. In addition there's a four-bedroom river house nearby plus a separate cottage.

Jenny Rice serves up a scrumptious buffet style menu that can be guaranteed to have something everyone will enjoy.

Jenny starts with homemade sourdough bread, soups (potato, chicken, Southwestern squash) and salad bar (veggie toss, slaw, cranberry relish, full salad bar, fruit salad, etc.) Then the roast beef with au jus, herb pork

roast with fried apples, meatloaf, chicken and rice, mashed potatoes, sweet potato casserole, stewed tomatoes, green beans and corn pudding.

May it be suggested that for dessert you try one of two: blackberry pie with a side of ice cream or the warm brownie with ice cream. Oh, what the heck, have them both.

The splendid décor and classy style of this inn reflects the florist background Jenny brings to this fantastic place to dine.

Traveling to Augusta is a destination unto its own, but for sure when

you do go you've got to eat here. It will be memorable. By the way, if you get there on Saturday night, there's a good chance a musical group will be performing between 6 p.m. and 8 p.m.

DINERS INFORMATION

Address:
103 W. 2nd Street
Hours:
Monday-Thursday, 11:45 a.m. – 7 p.m.
Friday-Saturday, 11:45 a.m. – 8 p.m.
Closed Sunday
Phone:
606-756-2667
Price Range: $$
Area Attractions:
Shops, Augusta Ferry, George Clooney home, Ohio River

Tousey House
BURLINGTON, KENTUCKY

Brad Wainscott carries on a family tradition with the Tousey House Tavern. The town of Burlington has the flavor of a little country village, and this two story 1822 structure fits in nicely.

"This has been a home, tavern, livery, boarding house, gift shop, consignment shop and a restaurant," offers general manager Eric Morehead.

But now, the white table clothes and napkins, punctuated by the heavy eating utensils, without question, give it an elegant country feel. And as nice as the Tousey House looks, the food is even better.

Appetizers here are quite an opening act. The made-daily soups, fried green tomatoes, shrimp & grits, Kentucky beer cheese served with warm pretzel bread, spinach & artichoke dip and catfish fingers are just a few.

Of course, there's a large assortment of salads and sandwiches, but it's the list of entrees that set this restaurant apart. The Wainscott family has a history of doing it right in the restaurant business and they certainly have done it here when it comes to their big city offerings. Chef's duck breast is served with country ham, roasted pears, endive, dried cranberries and a house-made pomegranate reduction. With this said you can only imagine

how good the bourbon & brown sugar pork tenderloin is, or the ribeye, or the walleye pike, or the Atlantic salmon, or the Alaskan halibut, or the fried chicken is.

The desserts are able to carry their end of this three-act performance of food. Vanilla bean crème Brule, and the pumpkin bread pudding with caramel sauce are just two of their delicious offerings.

The Tousey House Tavern offers a Sunday brunch that is equal to the task of holding its own with the regular menu. Banana bread French toast, eggs benedict, pancakes, hot browns, swanky Carolina shrimp & grits and fried chicken are just a few of your Sunday choices.

DINERS INFORMATION

Address:
5963 N. Jefferson
Hours:
Tuesday-Thursday, 11 a.m. – 9 p.m.
Friday-Saturday, 11 a.m. – 10 p.m.
Sunday, 10 a.m. – 8 p.m.
Closed Monday
Phone:
859-586-9900
Price Range: $$
Area Attractions:
Newport Aquarium, pro sports

Welch's Riverside Restaurant

CARROLLTON, KENTUCKY

When a restaurant opens up at 5 a.m., you know this is where the locals eat, and more often than not, they are waiting for the doors to be unlocked. And as might be expected, they all eat at their usual tables every day.

"Half of them say 'the same' when ordering," says Tammy, owner Donna Welch's sister, when taking their order. "They think they're solving the world's problems."

The view of the Ohio River from inside this restaurant is spectacular, so it's easy to see why this is a busy place. There is a boat tie-off just below Welch's where boaters can ease in, tie-off, and walk the gentle slope to the restaurant.

"We have several customers who come over from the Madison, Indiana area across the river," Tammy adds. "On the weekends we get several of them."

Welch's is a breakfast, lunch and dinner place with a full complement of omelets, bacon, sausage, pancakes, hashbrowns, grits and French toast. By the way, their morning offerings are served all day.

There's just about any kind of sandwich your heart desires as well as T-bone and ribeye steaks, country ham, fried chicken, shrimp, catfish and clams.

Daily customers have a choice of three different meats to choose from when it comes to the meat and two specials. Mashed potatoes, green beans, dried beans, and slaw are just a few of the sides.

Welch's Riverside opened on Thanksgiving Day in 1997 and thank goodness they did.

DINERS INFORMATION ?

Address:
505 Main Street
Hours:
Monday-Saturday, 5 a.m. – 8 p.m.
Sunday, 5 a.m. – 3 p.m.
Phone:
502-732-9118
Price Range: $
Area Attractions:
General Butler State Park; Ohio River

Bank 253	Pikeville, KY
Blue Raven	Pikeville, KY
Bruen's Restaurant	Stanton, KY
Carriage House Restaurant	Paintsville, KY
Carter Cave State Park	Olive Hill, KY
Dino's Italian Restaurant	Berea, KY
Dixie Café	Corbin, KY
Fuzzy Duck Café	Morehead, KY
Jenny Wiley State Park	Prestonsburg, KY
Lizzie B's Café	Prestonsburg, KY
Miguel's Pizza	Slade, KY
Old Town Grill	London, KY
Purdy's Coffee Company	Richmond, KY
Rosie's Restaurant	Rush, KY
Snug Hollow	Irvine, KY
Tree House Café & Bakery	Hazard, KY

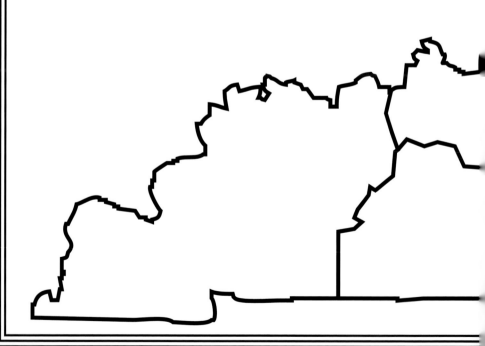

EASTERN REGION

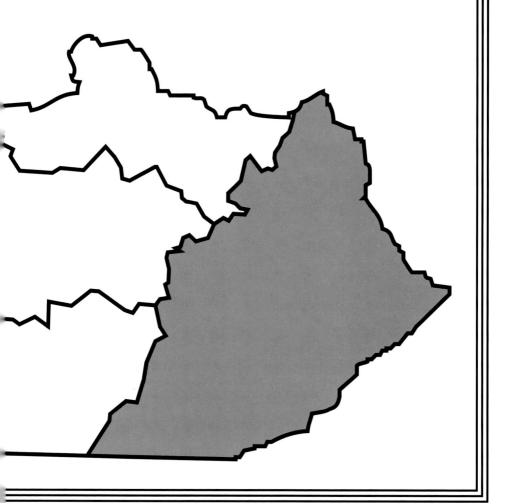

Bank 253

PIKEVILLE, KENTUCKY

If you guessed that this outstanding downtown Pikeville eatery is located in a former bank building, you are correct. Bank 253 has upped the ante with a restaurant that offers good food, not only for hungry patrons at lunch and dinner, but late night as well.

With appetizers that you might expect, such as nachos, wings, potato skins and fried pickles, sweet potato fries with sweet cream sauce, there are also Bavarian soft pretzels, sweet & sour shrimp, beer cheese, seared Ahi tuna, fried green tomatoes, and shrimp cocktail.

Salads, wraps and assorted sandwiches explode on the menu, but so, too, do other choices.

The made-in-house daily meatloaf is a keeper. Wrapped in bacon and placed atop whipped potatoes it is then topped with a demi-glaze and onion rings. Pay attention also to the chicken and waffles. It's a combination of their hand-made waffles and chicken tenders topped with a warm maple syrup. The hand-cut filets and ribeyes are popular, as is the salmon and blackened tuna mignon.

Bank 253 prides itself in specialty

drinks from its full service bar, such as the pixie-stix martini or a bloody Mary that is topped with a tator-tot, bacon, dill pickle and celery. That's what I'm talking about!

Do not, and it is repeated, *do not* leave here without the waffle sundae for dessert.

This restaurant doesn't roll up its sidewalk when nightfall arrives either. Live music is the norm on Thursday nights and on weekends late nights features DJ inspired sounds.

Address:
253 Second Street
Hours:
Monday-Wednesday, 11 a.m. – 11 p.m.
Thursday-Friday, 11 a.m. – 1 a.m.
Saturday, 11 a.m. – 2 a.m.
Phone:
606-432-6566
Price Range: $$
Things of Interest:
Pikeville cut-thru, Hatfield-McCoy Days, Hillbilly Days, Breaks State Park

EASTERN

Blue Raven

PIKEVILLE, KENTUCKY

When Chef Matt Corbin decided to open his Blue Raven Restaurant a few years ago, he wanted something that would appeal to both the more sophisticated diners as well as casual. He has done that with a menu that seems to offer something for everyone.

Matt has taken what was once a car dealership, big garage doors and all, and turned it into one fine eatery.

"I've used a lot of stuff that came from my family to decorate here," he says. "It seems to work."

And about that big garage door? In that area, an outdoor "patio" has been created with a simple "WA-LA". Raise the door and let the outside in.

There's no magic to the menu. It's simple and to the point.

With an offering that features such items as short rib biscuits, tempura fried shrimp, jumbo lump crab cakes, chicken and duck confit flatbread, and fried oysters, it's easy to see why customers drive from several counties away. And this is just the appetizers!

For the main course, how about the salmon mac and cheese? Then there's the salmon with a bourbon-soy glaze, jerk-rubbed pork tenderloin, herb-crusted lamb chops, filets and ribeyes.

For those who might want that casual choice with a cold beer, there are burgers, shrimp tacos, and delightful brisket sliders that

are topped with a sweet chili sauce, spicy ranch dressing, house pickles, onion straws and hand-cut fries.

There's much more to the Blue Raven than meets the eye ... like the made from scratch dressings, twice baked potatoes, and a kale salad.

A full service bar adds to the experience.

DINERS INFORMATION ❓

Address:
211 Main Street
Hours:
Tuesday-Friday, 11 a.m. – 2 p.m. (Lunch)
Tuesday-Saturday, 5 p.m. – 9 p.m. (Dinner)
Friday-Saturday, 5 p.m. – 10 p.m.
Phone:
606-509-2583
Price Range: $$
Area Attractions:
Pikeville cut-thru, Hatfield-McCoy Days, Hillbilly Days, Breaks State Park

Bruen's Restaurant

Bruen's is located just off of the Mountain Parkway in downtown Stanton, and just eyeballing it, the casual travelers probably wouldn't pull over unless recommended.

The block building, with the slanted tin roof, is not easy to find … but everybody in Stanton knows where it is, and in that regard it's easy to find after all.

Located in Powell County, this restaurant was first opened by Margaret Bruen according to some of the regulars who eat here as often as three times a day.

"I just got off the phone with one of our local historians, and he said there'd been a restaurant in this building since 1946," said one of the diners.

No matter what time of the day you visit Bruen's it might be difficult to find enough room to slip your car into a space. It's a happening place and that's the way owners Pam and Mike Helton like it.

"One customer from out of town called here to ask when we were open," said Kathleen, an employee. 'What are your hours?' he asked. From 4 'til 9, I answered. 'Oh, you are just a dinner place?' No, we're open from 4 a.m. 'til 9 p.m., seven days a week."

How early they open might depend on which waitress you talk to. One says 4 a.m., another says 4:30 a.m., but the front of the menu says 5 a.m. Anyway, it's early.

192

Kathy, the assistant manager, is proud that Bruen's try to serve only the freshest food possible.

"Our burgers are fresh, hand patted, not frozen," she says.

She is also vocal about the skillet fried chicken every Wednesday. "If you eat it with a knife and fork the locals might look at you kind of funny. Our daily specials include salmon patties, chicken and dumplings, baked chicken and fish on Friday," she adds.

This is a full menu eatery with a full-blown breakfast menu, as well as sandwiches, homemade vegetable soup and chili

Yes, there's a lot of local history in this little restaurant tucked in on a side street just off the main drag. Once called Jugtown until annexed into Stanton back in the '50s, Bruen's is a rediscovered treasure.

DINERS INFORMATION

Address:
8 Sipple Street
Hours:
Monday-Sunday, 4:30 a.m. — 9 p.m.
Phone:
606-663-4252
Price Range: $
Area Attractions:
Natural Bridge State Park, fall foliage, Red River Gorge

Carriage House Restaurant

PAINTSVILLE, KENTUCKY

For years the Carriage House, located in the Ramada Inn, has been a dining destination not only in Paintsville, but the entire area. It's dining in a classy setting at affordable prices.

The Carriage House Hotel opened in 1982 and became part of the Ramada program a few years ago. But the restaurant portion retained its original name.

The main dining room seats 100, and is a three-meal restaurant with breakfast, lunch and dinner. But it's those Sunday and special holiday buffets that are showstoppers. Served in the huge commons area, every table is a photo op.

Can you say chicken and dumplings', fried chicken, and cod fish? I thought you could.

"The fish is what everyone comes for," says a member of the waitstaff.

But don't count out the green beans, corn, macaroni, broccoli salad, slaw, potato salad or wild rice. It's all good.

And all of those desserts: honey bun cake, peanut butter, and butterscotch pies are just a few.

The menu in the main dining room offers a selection that might be expected at a place like this. Shrimp cocktail, and crab

cakes highlight a large selection of appetizers. Among the salads are Caesar, stuffed tomato, shrimp and fruits.

For the main course, prime rib, strip steak, ribeye, T-bone, and sirloin are served, as well as chops, and baby back ribs.

Chicken dishes, pasta and seafood round out a something-for-everyone restaurant. Pay attention to those Krab Kakes. The crab meat is blended with various spices and served with the restaurants special dipping sauce, hushpuppies, fries and coleslaw.

Address:
624 James Trimble Blvd.
Hours:
Monday-Saturday, 7 a.m. – 9 p.m.
Sunday, 8 a.m. – 8 p.m.
Phone:
606-789-4242
Price Range: $$
Area Attractions:
Loretta Lynn Homeplace (Butcher Hollow), U.S. 23 Country Music Highway, Mountain Home Place, Paintsville Lake.

Carter Cave State Park

Just because Carter Cave is one of the smaller resort parks in Kentucky, doesn't mean it has any less beauty. Its four remote caves are open for tours at different times of the year, and there's also enough full range of above-ground activities to keep a family entertained.

The Tierney Cavern Restaurant, located in the main lodge, is a three-meal a day facility, with a full menu and buffet style selections.

The restaurant has its own specialties not necessarily served at other parks: the baked fish, ribeye steak, Kentucky cordon bleu, grilled salmon, and pork chops. And then there are the Tierney Little "T" sandwiches. (The restaurant named in honor of John Tierney, a park naturalist for 30 years.) There's the Little T cheeseburger, catfish, chicken and southwestern chicken, all minis, served in threes on buttered rolls.

Carter Cave is open year-round with 28 guest rooms and eleven cottages. A nine-hole golf course is offered as is swimming, horseback riding, miniature golf, hiking, canoeing, fishing, and gem-mining for the kids.

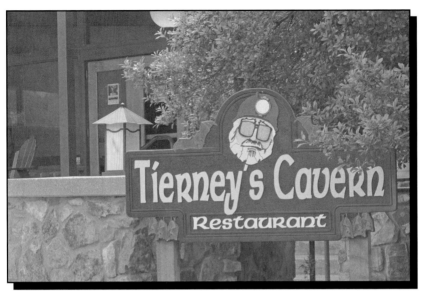

One of the annual highlights at Carter Cave is the "Winter Adventure Weekend" held the last full weekend of each January. Repelling, hiking, canoeing, and walking cave tours are a part of it all.

EASTERN

DINERS INFORMATION

Address:
344 Caveland Drive (I-64, exit 161)
Hours:
Daily, 7 a.m. — 10 a.m. (Breakfast); 11:30 a.m. — 2 p.m. (Lunch)
Monday-Thursday, 5 p.m. — 8 p.m.
Friday-Saturday, 5 p.m. — 9 p.m.
Sunday, 7 a.m. — 3 p.m.
Phone:
606-286-4411
Price Range: $$
Area Attractions:
Caves

Dino's Italian Restaurant

BEREA, KENTUCKY

When Dino Alexiou opened his eatery in Berea, he brought with him an infusion of cultures that have influenced the food he serves.

Born in Greece, growing up in Detroit and working in the food industry in North Carolina and then in Knoxville, Tennessee, he decided it was time to come to Kentucky.

Dino's may not be classified as fine dining, but it's a wonderful place to eat fine food.

"We buy the best quality cheese and flour," Dino offers. "We do everything we can do from scratch. I don't like frozen."

This restaurant has a clean, crisp look upon entering, and a welcoming step-up-and-order counter with an easy to read menu behind it. This allows customers to explore the surprisingly large array of offerings in a restaurant this small.

Salads, hot and cold hoagies, burgers, hot melts, calzones, Stromboli's, Greek pita wraps are all part of the dining scene here. But so is the spaghetti.

"We offer a special every day on our spaghetti," Dino says.

However, if you want to step it up a notch with the spaghetti, you have a choice of baked spaghetti, spaghetti pie, or spaghetti Alfredo, chicken Alfredo, eggplant parmigiana, veal parmigiana, and on and on.

But what Dino's has really made a name for is their pizza, and there are too many combos to list here. It's sort of like if you can imagine it, they have it.

Perhaps the Italian fare is not what you want, but be assured you won't go hungry here. Pork chops, chicken breast, chopped steak, gyro meat platter, mixed grill and even catfish all add to the power of the menu.

DINERS INFORMATION

Address:
1300 Walnut Meadow Road (Exit 77-I-75)
Hours:
Monday-Thursday, 11 a.m. — 10:30 p.m.
Friday-Saturday, 11 a.m. — 11:30 p.m.
Sunday, 11 a.m. — 10 p.m.
Phone:
859-228-0001
Price Range: $
Area Attractions:
Artisian Center, world-class arts and crafts, Berea College

Dixie Café

CORBIN, KENTUCKY

Almost anyone who has ever been in downtown Corbin has heard of the Dixie, and there's even a good chance they've eaten there.

The restaurant is closely tied to the legendary Redhound sports history of the community, where the teams and fans gathered after the games to, more often than not, celebrate a victory.

Ed and Carolyn Garr, several years ago, decided to keep the Dixie alive, and today they are keeping the tradition going.

"We try to keep it like the old-timers remember it when they come back home," says Ed. "Plus, we've added some new and even improved on the old."

The Dixie's décor hasn't changed much over the last few decades, but that's what makes this a special place to eat. When you visit, take a look around. You'll see some pictures of past sports teams, and even a state championship trophy or two. There's even a photo op outside the building. It's the original painted logo of the great Corbin High School Redhound.

Anyone who has ever eaten here knows the Dixie's reputation for its famous chili buns and chilidogs.

"Anytime any of us go back to Corbin, our first stop is the Dixie," said Bill "Yogi" Meadors, who played on some of the best Redhound football teams back in the '50s.

"You can't go back to Corbin and not go to the Dixie," says Rodger Bird, a former UK football All-American who played in Super Bowl II for the Oakland Raiders.

The Dixie is mainly a breakfast and lunch place.

For breakfast, if you're hungry, you'll want to order Ed's Breakfast Special. It's two pancakes, two eggs, bacon or sausage, hashbrowns and a drink. Country ham and tenderloin are also served as well as biscuits and gravy.

Plate lunches of chicken tenders, meatloaf, and country fried steak, catfish, and chopped steak are all popular items.

There is a lot going on in a good way in this legendary eatery in downtown Corbin.

Fuzzy Duck Café

MOREHEAD, KENTUCKY

The name alone gets your attention. And once you get there, you'll be glad you did. Located in downtown Morehead, just around the corner from Morehead State University, this coffee shop-grill has quickly become a hangout place for all age groups.

The uniqueness of the Fuzzy Duck is that it is located in what was the lobby of the old University Cinema, and it works. Tastefully arranged tables and chairs surround a step-up counter, where coffee and food can be ordered.

What makes this place even more special is the large Coffee Tree Book Store in the main seating portion of the old theater. Of course, the seats have been removed and the flooring has been terraced for a smooth transition for shoppers. The theater stage is still in place and makes for the perfect area for various programs.

The Fuzzy Duck prides itself in its coffee drinks of various concoctions, but also popular are its spreads: chicken salad, pimento cheese, olive nut and Benedictine.

The business is a joint operation between Dan and Marge Thomas and daughter, Susan and her husband, Thomas Grant.

Sandwiches, wraps and hot grill choices dot the menu, as well as delicious soups.

This is just a cool place to visit, and if it's hot outside an iced ginger peach or raspberry tea may be suggested.

DINERS INFORMATION

Address:
159 E. Main Street
Hours:
Monday-Saturday, 7 a.m. – 8 p.m.
Closed Sunday
Phone:
606-784-9877
Price Range: $
Area Attractions:
Morehead State University; Carter Cave State Park

EASTERN

Jenny Wiley State Park

Jenny Wiley is one of those Kentucky State Parks that just keeps getting better and better each time you return. And so does the food.

The park became part of the state's system in 1954, and nearby Dewey Lake offers visitors a magnificent view of the marina. The lake itself is more than 18-miles long and has 52-miles of shoreline.

The dining room that seats well over 200 is located in May Lodge, which offers 49 rooms in seclusion surrounded by towering pines and scenic mountains. There also are 18 cottages close by.

An assortment of appetizers, soups, salads and sandwiches are good choices, but so are the entrée items. The hot brown, featuring Kentucky country ham, is as good as you'll taste anywhere. And what makes all of Kentucky's parks special is their involvement with the Kentucky Proud program in which the parks chefs utilize state grown and raised food products in their day-to-day operation. That's why the country ham is the real deal along with Purnell sausage, John Conti Coffee and all of the milk products.

Diners can't go wrong with the Cajun grilled fish or the huge serving of catfish filet. This is a dish that can easily be divided.

The Reuben, grilled marbled rye with slices of corned beef, melted Swiss, sauerkraut, topped with Thousand Island dressing is a great choice.

The Dewey Grill and the back patio really come alive with the weekly "After 5 Friday" event. Local groups sing and play music and visitors can order from a bar menu that includes half-price appetizers.

The Dewey Grill breakfast here is usually offered from a buffet with lots of choices or there's a full menu to order from.

The park also features Jenny Wiley Theatre for the performing arts through professionally produced musicals. There's also an executive 9-hole golf course. But one of the most popular attractions here is the Elk Tour. Convenient van travel is arranged to see these huge animals as they roam about in a habitat they were reintroduced to back in 1997. The herd is said to number well over 10,000 today.

DINERS INFORMATION

Directions:
75 Theatre Court
Hours:
Daily, 7 a.m — 10 a.m. (Breakfast); 11 a.m. — 2 p.m. (Lunch);
    5 p.m. — 9 p.m. (Dinner)
Dewey Grill, 3 p.m. — 10 p.m.
Phone:
606-889-1790
Price Range: $$
Area Attractions:
Elk tours, Dewey Lake, Stonecrest Golf Course, Jenny Wiley Theatre, Ranier Racing Exhibit (located in Visitor Center), Legendary tourism director Fred James.

Lizzie B's Café

PRESTONSBURG, KENTUCKY

This is a fast paced restaurant. If you don't believe it, just visit on Thursday, Friday or Saturday nights.

Visitors here might not expect to find a Hawaii-California themed eatery in Prestonsburg, but that's what Tim has done and he hasn't looked back.

"The breads are what make our place rock," says owner Tim Branham, who named his restaurant after his daughter.

"A friend of mine, Anna, had the Waialua Bakery on the North Shore in Hawaii, when I lived there, and she gave me several of the wonderful recipes we use here," he offered.

The dark handmade woodwork, mahogany bar and Indonesian tables and chairs have created just the ambience Tim was looking for.

"We grill our burgers and steaks, and we keep as much of our menu away from the fryer as possible," he adds.

Soups and salads are popular here, and the sandwiches and wraps are the real deal. Lizzie B's offers their sandwiches in half or full orders, depending on your appetite. Steaks, chops, prime rib, spaghetti and pizza are also offered.

"We cook everything to order," says Tim. "And our meats are fresh and the turkey we serve is pulled from the bone."

The restaurant is something for everyone, from a full-fledged coffee shop with special treat smoothies, to a baked-goodie case with cookies, cinnamon rolls and cheesecakes, to an extensive wine list, to a newly opened micro-brewery right there on the property.

Entertainment plays on weekends.

Address:
2010 KY Route 321159, E. Main Street
Hours:
Monday-Wednesday, 10:30 a.m. – 9:30 p.m.
Thursday-Saturday, 10:30 a.m. – late
Closed Sunday
Phone:
606-886-2844
Price Range: $$
Area Attractions:
Jenny Wiley State Park, Mountain Arts Center, Dewey Lake, Moonshine Tours, Ranier Racing Exhibit.

Miguel's Pizza

SLADE, KENTUCKY

This is one of the most unique restaurants in these pages. Not only is the pizza really good, but it also sits smack dab in the middle of Natural Bridge State Resort Park, that is a part of the Red River Gorge.

Miguel's Pizza is owned and operated by Miguel Ventura and his wife Susan, and along with son Dario, have turned this little yellow roadside place into a world known place to not only eat pizza, but also to camp and get ready to strike out on major league hikes and gorge climbs.

"In 2007, a company from France held a big event here and the publicity from it put us on the world-wide map," says Susan Ventura.

There's a lot that goes on here at Miguel's, with camp sites, room rentals, and cabin rentals, but one of the biggest is the pizza.

You can be sure there is no combination of pizzas that you can think up that you can't get here.

USA Today named Miguel's as one of "51 Great Pizza Parlors Worth a Detour."

The handmade crust and homemade sauce is the foundation of the more than 45 fresh and tasty toppings for the pizzas.

As big as pizza is here ... and it's big, Miguel's also serves up ribeye steaks, BBQ and BLT's. And breakfast, well believe it or not, you can get the traditional eggs, bacon and potatoes, but also omelets with a choice of 45 toppings.

Miguel's Pizza, from its humbling beginnings in 1984, has matured into rock star status. Miguel, born in Portugal in a family of bakers, has used his talents of a self-taught artist that took him from California to Connecticut and finally to Slade, Kentucky, where he and Susan took an old run down building on Kentucky Hwy. 11 and turned it into a legendary little pizza place.

Old Town Grill

This stand-alone restaurant seems to pop up out of nowhere in the old established Dog Patch Trading Center, just off I-75 at exit 41.

Brian Carpenter and Mike Caffrey have put together an extensive menu that has led to the restaurant being voted London's best.

You almost don't know where to start when you pick up the menu. From the potato skin bites covered in ranch dressing, diced tomatoes, cheese, bacon and sour cream, this starter sets the stage for things to follow.

Sandwiches, soups, salads, steaks (sirloins, New York strip, chopped), prime rib, smoked pork loin, smoked beef brisket, barbeque ribs, and hand-pulled pork barbeque dinners are featured items.

Old Town also serves Italian fare: spaghetti marinara, blackened chicken pasta, fettuccine alfredo, baked spaghetti and shrimp bake.

Of course, a place like this offers chicken and seafood dishes that includes a marinated chicken breast, grilled chicken, salmon, grilled crab cakes, shrimp tilapia and catfish.

A special lunch menu is a huge draw here and is available from 11 a.m.-3 p.m., Monday-Friday, with your order guaranteed in 15 minutes or less ... or it's free.

Old Town Grill has a separate full service bar that is also quite popular in the area.

This is a family friendly restaurant that offers something for everyone regardless of what you are hungry for. The parking lot begins to fill up just before the doors open at 11 a.m.

Address:
25 Dogpatch Trading Center (I-75, Exit 41)
Hours:
Sunday-Thursday, 11 a.m. – 10:00 p.m.
Friday-Saturday, 11 a.m. – 11 p.m.
Closed Sunday
Phone:
606-862-1684
Price Range: $$
Area Attractions:
Levi Jackson State Park, Chicken Festival

Purdy's Coffee Company

RICHMOND, KENTUCKY

In 2011 Kristen and Robert Purdy, along with several family members, jumped into the coffee and restaurant business in downtown Richmond with both feet.

Taking an old historic building that over the years had housed Irene's Dress Shop, Lane's Jewelry, Noland's Beauty Shop and another restaurant, they worked for over a year to restore the quality accents of a tin ceiling and hardwood floors that strongly hint of days gone by.

"Robert and I met at Murray State University," says Kristen. "He was on the rifle team and I was on the rowing team. After college, he came to Richmond for the State Police Academy. When we married, we decided if we had the chance this is where we wanted to live. We fell in love with this place."

From the time Purdy's opens their door in the morning until they close at night, there is constant traffic in and out for the selections of coffees, bagels, quiches, muffins, chicken salad, pesto turkey melt, and the delicious Pollo Purdy, a spicy pulled chicken with chipotle sauce, cheddar and then Panini grilled. Salads are also served.

The dessert choices include brownie squares, cookies, peanut butter bars, and caramel apple Danish.

Purdy's is a great place to relax and enjoy some good food. It's also a good place to flip open the laptop, or read in a comfortable setting with a perfect cup of coffee.

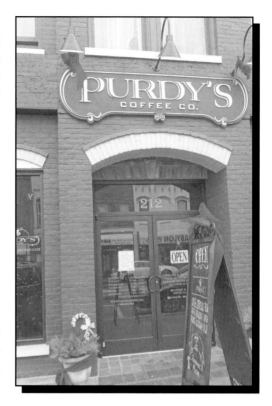

DINERS INFORMATION

Address:
212 W. Main Street
Hours:
Monday-Thursday, 7 a.m. – 9 p.m.
Friday-Saturday, 7 a.m. – 7 p.m.
Closed Sunday
Phone:
859-624-9920
Price Range: $
Area Attractions:
Eastern Kentucky University, Bybee Pottery

Rosie's Restaurant

RUSH, KENTUCKY

This Boyd County restaurant, that looks like it might have been a service station years ago several miles from Ashland, is what country eating is all about.

"Rosie's is pretty much Rush," said one customer in describing how big a community Rush is.

The restaurant seats about 48, and paper towels in a handy dispenser serve as the napkins at each table. For sure, there is nothing fancy here. It's just a foodie place off the beaten path to eat. Rosie's is a 24-hour a day eatery, never closing and employing three shifts, and breakfast is served all day, every day. There's not much this restaurant, that might be described as a "hole-in-the-wall," doesn't serve.

Ham and eggs, pancakes, bacon, omelets, biscuit sandwiches, soups, salads, burgers, BLTs, Philly steak, clubs, roast beef, fried chicken, pork chops, open-face roast beef, spaghetti, and last but certainly not least is the Big 'Ole Mess & Cornbread. (Polish sausage, fried potatoes, onions, and peppers sautéed together, all served with a bowl of brown beans).

Rosie's has a kids menu for 10-and-under.

A sign on the wall reads "sit, relax and gossip", and that's exactly what many of the locals do. "This is my second time in here today," laughed one customer.

One of the most popular items is the chicken and dumplings. And so is the smoked pork chop served with green beans, mashed potatoes and cornbread.

One could go on and on about the depth of the menu for such a little restaurant, but some of the sides have got to be mentioned: baked potato, kale, mac-n-cheese, stewed tomatoes, carrots and more.

If you're not hungry for a full meal, stop by for a slice of the banana split cake, chocolate or peanut butter pie.

Rosie's is worth the hunt.

Address:
8869 U.S. 60
Hours:
Never closes!
Phone:
606-928-3547
Price Range: $
Area Attractions:
Carter Cave State Park

Snug Hollow

IRVINE, KENTUCKY

Barbara Napier calls her Snug Hollow Farm Bed & Breakfast "holler hospitality," and after one visit here it's easy to see why.

Sitting on 300 acres not far from Berea, not only does this wonderful get-a-way retreat offer relaxing overnight accommodations in a spacious two-story log structure, but Barbara also serves up some unique gourmet vegetarian lunches and dinners for those who want to only dine. All it takes is a quick phone call to make your reservation.

Barbara promotes her menu as organic and her meals of fresh produce, tasty soups, creamy gourmet pastas, homemade breads, and oven-hot homemade pies will make you want to eat here time and again.

The meals are served on a screened porch with a beautiful view of the wildflowers and grazing wildlife. When the season turns cooler, a warm fire not far from your table makes for a warm-fuzzy dining experience.

Even though it's not classified as a gated community, you still might have to pass through a one — a cattle gate — to get to Snug Hollow. This is what makes a visit here so unique. Be sure and close the gate behind you.

Barbara's place has been recognized in several national publications.

There's even a 155-year-old Chestnut log cabin next to the big house, for those who might want to lodge in a bit more privacy. Its own private porch and tin roof are perfect for a rainy afternoon.

Snug Hollow sits just off Red Lick Road on McSwain Branch about eight miles from Irvine and 20 county miles from Berea.

DINERS INFORMATION

Address:
790 McSwain Branch
Hours:
Call for reservations
Phone:
606-723-4786
Price Range: $$
Area Attractions:
The Kentucky Artisan Center, Arts & Crafts, Berea College

EASTERN

Tree House Café & Bakery

HAZARD, KENTUCKY

What Jenn Noble has done with her downtown restaurant in Hazard is completely out of the norm from other local places.

"I started out wanting to be an artist," says Jenn. "But then I decided I wanted to come back home and try to make a difference in revitalizing downtown."

Here the food is organic, but that doesn't mean it's not good. Because it is!

Burgers, patty melts are served, but perhaps not in the traditional way. There's the fried egg burger, the smokehouse, and the palm burger with grilled pineapple, coconut, American, Swiss and provolone cheeses beneath a sweet and sour sauce served on a brioche bun.

But there's much more: Philly cheesesteak, Cuban, vegetarian, Pablo black bacon grilled cheese, Reuben and more. But wait, there's more, with seven different chicken and turkey sandwiches to choose from.

Jenn offers pizzas, all of which are baked on tandoori bread.

She says the most popular seller at the Tree House is the Italian Panini. Made up of ham, salami, pepperoni, bacon, tomato, lettuce and Swiss cheese, this sandwich is as good as it gets.

Notice part of the Tree House name is bakery, and it does not disappoint with cakes, cupcakes and sundry items.

The 100-seat restaurant offers little nooks with couches and chairs to nibble on food and have conversations.

"I wanted to create a place where people could escape to relax, be comfortable and cozy," Jenn added.

It's also more than just food here. Poetry night, music night, local art are all part of the unique experience.

DINERS INFORMATION

Address:
426 Main Street
Hours:
Monday-Friday, 11 a.m. — 9 p.m.
Saturday, 3 p.m. — 9 p.m.
Closed Sunday
Phone:
606-487-1931
Price Range: $
Area Attractions:
Buckhorn Lake

EASTERN

219

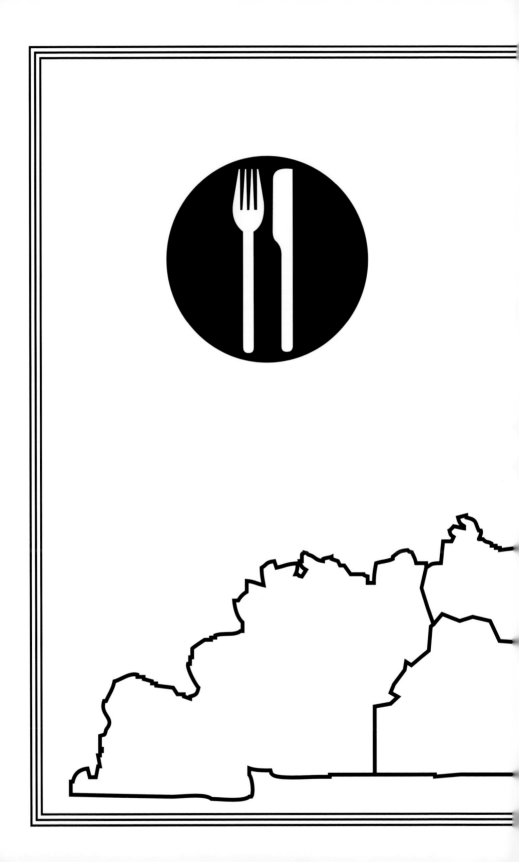

RECIPES

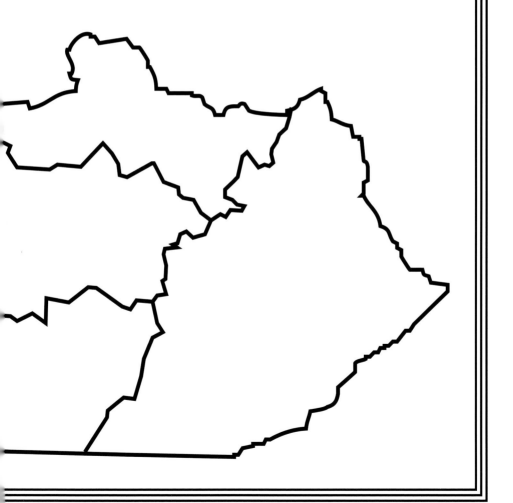

Soups, Salads & Starters

Beef Barley Soup

5 gallon beef stock
1 gallon celery, diced
1 gallon onion, diced
2 quarts barley pearls
2 lbs. beef base
½ cup Worcestershire sauce

10 lbs. beef scraps
3 #10 cans diced carrots
3 Tbl. black pepper
2 Tbl. salt
1 quart Chef Bouquet

In a 10 gallon pot, place beef stock, celery, onions, barley, beef base, Worcestershire sauce, black pepper and salt. Cook until vegetables and barley are tender.

Place the beef scraps in a 4-inch steam table pan and cover with foil. Bake slowly until the meat reaches a temp of 145 degrees. Add to 10 Gallon pot.

In a 5 gallon pot, bring the diced carrots to a boil.

Slowly add Chef Bouquet to the 10 gallon pot until the liquid turns the color of walnut.

Mix ingredients from all pots together until thoroughly mixed.

Separate into portions to store properly.

Courtesy of Colonial Cottage Inn, Erlanger, Kentucky.

Coleslaw

½ cup mayonnaise
½ cup powdered sugar
9 Tbl. red wine vinegar

Mix mayonnaise, sugar and red wine vinegar together before serving so that the dressing does not get diluted from the water that leaches out of the slaw mix as it sits. Enjoy!

Courtesy of Stinky and Coco's, Winchester, Kentucky.

Fried Banana Peppers

Whole banana peppers
Buttermilk
Wiesenberger fish batter
Eggs

De-seed whole hot banana peppers and cut in half. Soak in buttermilk
for an hour. Pre-bread the peppers using Wiesenberger Fish batter and
place on wax paper. Refrigerate overnight.

When ready to fry the peppers use an egg wash and re-bread with the dry
fish batter. This will ensure that the coating will stick to the peppers.
Put breaded peppers in fryer for about three minutes at 350 degrees.
They will turn a golden brown. Serve with cocktail sauce.

Courtesy of A.P. Suggins Bar & Grill, Lexington, Kentucky.

Goat Cheese Salad
with Honey Pistachio Vinaigrette

This is hands down one of our best sellers and certainly our best-selling
salad. We toss the vinaigrette with spring mix, thinly sliced red onion
and cucumber before topping with the fried goat cheese medallions and
crushed pistachios.

Goat Cheese Medallions

10.5 oz. goat cheese, room temp
4 oz. cream cheese, room temp
Panko bread crumbs, flour and egg wash for breading
Oil for frying

Mix the goat cheese and cream cheese in a stand mixer with a whisk
attachment until well incorporated and smooth.

Use a small ice cream scoop to portion the goat cheese mixture into
a pan of flour and place in the refrigerator to chill for 30 minutes.
Remove from the refrigerator and roll in the flour before shaping
into small discs or cakes (similar to a crab cake).

Next place the medallions in the egg wash and finally roll them in some
panko bread crumbs or any kind of bread crumb.

Shallow fry the medallions on the stove or counter top fryer at 350 or
375 degrees until golden brown. Be careful not to leave in too long
because the cheese will begin to ooze.

Honey Pistachio Vinaigrette

½ cup pistachios
1 Tbl. Dijon mustard
8 oz. honey (local)
½ cup warm water, plus more if needed
1 lemon zest then juiced
Canola Oil or salad oil to desired consistency

Using a blender or food processor blend the pistachios, Dijon mustard, warm water and pinch of salt/pepper until smooth. Add honey and lemon zest/juice to the blender and continue blending. With the blender on high, slowly pour in the oil until the dressing is the consistency of vinaigrette.

The dressing will thicken once cooled in the refrigerator, but can be left at room temperature.

Courtesy of Blue Raven, Pikeville, Kentucky.

Gumbo

4 chicken breasts (diced)
1 link sausage (diced)
(Seafood if you like)
1 onion
1 bell pepper
Rice

Roux – Flour and oil browned real well, or you can buy it in a jar.

Take a stock pot, put sausage, chicken, onion and bell pepper, and creole seasoning.

Fill pot with water and let boil.

Add roux to make it as brown as you like. Cook rice on the side and put in bowl and add Gumbo.

Courtesy of Margie's Southern Café, Maysville, Kentucky.

Lettuce Wraps

2 lbs. Chicken – roasted and chopped
½ cup fresh chopped mushrooms
½ cup water chestnuts, chopped
¼ cup green onion, chopped
½ cup Kalbi sauce
Salt & pepper to taste

Prepare chicken as instructed.

Add all other ingredients. Simmer low to medium heat until veggies are fork tender.

Garnish with chow mein noodles and green onions.

Serve with lettuce cups and warm Kalbi.

Yields – four (4)

Courtesy of The Crowded House, Madisonville, Kentucky.

Summer Salad

2 quarts broccoli
1 head cauliflower
6-8 slices cooked crispy bacon,
    crumbled
½ cup chopped red onion
½ cup shredded carrots

½ cup raisins (optional)
½ cup sunflower kernels
1 cup cherry tomatoes, halved
8 oz. sharp cheddar, cut into very
    small chunks
2 cups sweet dressing (listed below)

Sweet Dressing

1 ½ cups sugar
¾ cup vinegar
1 gal. Kraft heavy mayo
1 tsp. salt
1 tsp. pepper

Put ingredients in a bowl and stir together.

Courtesy of Parcell's Deli & Grill, Benton, Kentucky.

Taco Soup

1 lb. lean ground beef or turkey
¼ cup chopped onion
1 46 oz. can tomato juice
1 10 oz. can Rotel or other brand with green chiles
1 14-16 oz. black beans
1 14-16 oz. corn
1 14-16 oz. chili beans
1 14-16 oz. pinto beans
1 pkg. Hidden Valley ranch dressing mix
1 pkg. taco seasoning mix
Sour Cream, shredded cheese and tortilla chips for garnishing

Combine the meat and onion in a large heavy pot over medium heat.
    Brown the meat breaking it up as it cooks. Drain any excess fat.
Add the tomato juice and the next 7 ingredients. Stir well and bring to
    a boil. Reduce heat and simmer for 30 minutes.
Serve hot and garnish with sour cream, shredded cheese and tortilla
    chips as desired. Serves 8-10.

Courtesy of Annie Ruby's, Burkesville, Kentucky.

Tomato Basil Soup

1 gallon can crushed tomatoes
1 cup chopped basil
2 Tbls. garlic
2 Tbls. Minors vegetable base
Salt & pepper to taste
1 cup heavy cream

Stir together first five ingredients. Bring to a boil over medium high heat. Simmer for 15 minutes. Stir in heavy cream. Puree with an immersion blender.

Courtesy of Wild Mountain Bakery, Murray, Kentucky.

Vinegar Slaw
(Makes 5 gallons)

10 lbs. cabbage
1 ½- 2 cups finely chopped onion
3 Tbls. salt
15 cups vinegar
7 cups vegetable oil
Dash red pepper
1 ½ tsp. minced garlic
3 Tbls. Dijon mustard
12 cups sugar
2 Tbls. pepper

Mix cabbage, onions and salt in a large bowl.
Combine remaining ingredients in a large stockpot and bring to a boil. After cooking, remove from heat to cool. When cool, pour over cabbage mixture and mix well.
A big hit in Hazel!

Courtesy of Blue & White Grill, Hazel, Kentucky.

Sauces & Dressings

Bleu Cheese Dressing

5 lbs. Bleu Cheese crumbles
½ gallon mayo
2 ½ lbs. sour cream
¼ gallon buttermilk
¼ cup chopped garlic
½ cup red wine vinegar
2 Tbl. salt & pepper mix
¼ cup sugar

Place all ingredients in a large bowl.
Blend until the bleu cheese is the size of a pea.
Makes approximately six quarts.

Courtesy of Guthrie's River House, Burnside, Kentucky.

Bourbon Alfredo Sauce

½ cup unsalted butter
1 cup heavy cream (whipping cream)
2 cups Parmesan cheese
Pinch or two of salt & pepper
Pinch nutmeg
Splash bourbon

Mix all together.

Courtesy of Ariella Bistro & Bar, Russellville, Kentucky.

Bourbon Blueberry Sauce

1 Tbls. chopped garlic & shallot
3 Tbls. olive oil
½ cup bourbon
2 cups fresh blueberries
¼ cup packed brown sugar
1 Tbls. chopped fresh parsley

1 Tbls. Balsamic vinegar
1 tsp. minced fresh thyme

Sauté chopped shallot and garlic in oil over medium heat until soft, about 5 minutes. Slowly add bourbon and increase heat to high and bring to a boil.

Once most of the liquid has evaporated, stir in blueberries, balsamic vinegar, brown sugar and return to a boil. Reduce heat and simmer, stirring occasionally until desired thickness. Season with salt and pepper.

Serve over pork, steak or fish.

Courtesy of The Miller House, Owensboro, Kentucky.

White Lightnin' Sauce
(Great for chicken and turkey)

1 gallon Hellman's mayonnaise
4 cups cider vinegar
¼ cup fresh lemon juice
3 Tbl. onion powder
3 Tbl. garlic powder
1 Tbl. cayenne pepper
3 Tbl. black pepper

Wisk together mayonnaise, vinegar and lemon juice until smooth. Add spices slowly and mix thoroughly together.

Cover and refrigerate until ready to use.

Courtesy of Shack in the Back, Fairdale, Kentucky.

Champagne Honey Vinaigrette Salad Dressing

2 oz. orange blossom honey
3 oz. chopped shallots
1/2 cup Champagne vinegar
1/2 cup Chardonnay Wine (we recommend Kendall-Jackson)
1 tsp. pepper (to taste)
1 tsp. kosher salt (to taste)
1 Tbl. fresh minced parsley
1 cup olive oil

Combine all ingredients except the oil in a blender or food processor. Blend, adding the oil in a steady stream down the center of the vortex until completely emulsified. Keeps in the refrigerator for up to 7 days.

Courtesy of Ricardo's, Versailles, Kentucky.

Drinks

Caramel Mocha Jo

12 oz. coffee
3 Tbl. mocha
½ oz. caramel monin syrup
1 small creamer

Mix together, and top with whipped cream.
Courtesy of Fuzzy Duck, Morehead, Kentucky.

Sleigh Ride
(holiday drink)

12 oz. coffee
3 Tbl. mocha
½ oz. Monin peppermint syrup

Mix together, and top with whipped cream and pieces of peppermint.
Courtesy of Fuzzy Duck, Morehead, Kentucky.

Main Dishes

The Autumn Sandwich

3 - 4 oz. fresh white turkey, sliced thinly along the grain
Cranberry walnut bread (or similar seasonal bread)
Green apple. Sliced as thinly as you can
Fresh apricot preserves
Swiss cheese

Courtesy of Tree House, Hazard, Kentucky.

Baked Tenderloin

6 lbs. sliced and tenderized tenderloin
Self-rising flour
Water
Kitchen bouquet brown & seasoning
Large skillet
Medium sized deep-side baking pan or dish

Prepare a skillet with ¼ inch oil and heat to medium-high, but not to the point of smoking. Dredge a piece of tenderloin liberally in flour, shake off excess. (Note: Do not use milk batter, flour only). Then put the tenderloin in hot oil. Cook and turn until the flour browns on each side. (Don't worry if it doesn't seem as if it cooks long enough to cook through. It will finish cooking during the second step. You are just browning the flour during this step). Continue until all of your tenderloin is cooked. Don't clean out your pan, you will need the grease.

Next, prepare your gravy. Heat the remaining grease in your pan to medium heat. Add approximately ½ cup flour to your grease and stir until it browns. Depending on the size of skillet you are using, add 8-12 cups of cold water. Remember to add the water quickly! Stir out any clumps of four and continue stirring until the mixture comes to a boil. If the gravy becomes thick just add more water. You want it to stay watery, as it will thicken-up in the oven. Add kitchen bouquet very sparingly until medium brown is reached. Add salt & pepper to taste. Switch to low heat and keep stirring until ready to use.

Preheat oven to 400 degrees.

Using a ladle, add a thin coat of gravy to the bottom of your baking pan. Then add a layer of the tenderloin. Add gravy until your first layer of tenderloin is covered. Then add the second layer of tenderloin; again cover with gravy. Repeat until all of the tenderloin is in the pan. Make sure all of the meat is covered in gravy.

Cover the pan with foil and put it in the oven for one hour!

Courtesy of Coe's, Russell Springs, Kentucky.

Beef Tips/Noodles

1pkg. egg noodles
1 pkg. stew meat
1 med. Onion
2 celery sticks
garlic

Brown onions in pot with olive oil. Add diced celery. Add meat and cover with water, salt and pepper and a little garlic. Cook for two hours. If the consistency is too thick, just add water.

Cook noodles according to package directions. Drain and set aside.

When finished, pour over top of drained noodles.

Courtesy of Angelo's, Independence, Kentucky.

Chili

5 lbs. ground beef
¼ cup chili powder
2 Tbl. salt
2 Tbl. minced garlic
1 Tbl. cumin
2 Tbl. sugar
1 bell pepper, diced
1 white onion
1 16 oz. chili beans
1 16 oz. diced tomatoes
1 16 oz. tomato sauce
4 cups water
1 Dark Hershey Bar

Put ground beef and 2 cups water in stock pan. Place on high until the meat is well-drained. Strain meat about 5 minutes. Place meat back in stockpot, add rest of the ingredients and mix well.

Place the pan back on stove and let simmer on medium-low for a minimum of 30 minutes.

Courtesy of Doe's Eat Place, Paducah, Kentucky.

Crab Cakes

¼ cup mayonnaise
¼ juice of whole lemon
1 Tbl. dark mustard
1 tsp. Old Bay seasoning
Butter crackers
1 lb. crab

Mix into a patty and fry in skillet with a little olive oil.

Clay's Downtown, Paris, Kentucky.

Fish Tacos

6 oz. fresh fish (tuna or mahi)
1 cup shredded cabbage (lettuce may be substituted)
¼ cup pico de gallo
2 Tbl. spicy mayo
2 flour tortillas
Shredded cheese (optional)

Spicy Mayo
4 Tbl. mayo
1 ½ Tsp. blackening seasoning (to taste)

Cook fish to your desired method (fried, grilled, blackened)
Warm tortillas and add shredded cabbage, or lettuce, and pico. Place cooked fish on top of pico and drizzle with spicy mayo. Top with cheese (optional).

Courtesy of Fishtales, Nancy, Kentucky.

Grilled Chicken Pasta Bake with Mornay Sauce

3 Tbl. butter
3 Tbl. flour
2 ½ cups milk
Salt
Freshly ground white pepper
Pinch nutmeg
6 oz. Parmigiano-Reggiano cheese, grated

2 Tbl. olive oil
1 large fennel bulb, cored and thinly sliced
Freshly ground black pepper
2 lbs. chicken breast, cooked
1 lb. ziti pasta, cooked al dente
¼ cup fresh basil, chiffonaded

In a medium saucepan over medium heat, melt the butter. Stir in the flour and cook for 2 minutes. Whisk in the milk, 1/2 cup at a time. Season with salt, pepper and nutmeg. Cook, stirring constantly for 4-6 minutes. Remove from the heat and whisk in ½ cup of the grated cheese. Set aside and keep warm.

In a large mixing bowl, combine the pasta, chicken mixture and Mornay sauce. Mix well. Pour into a greased baking dish. Sprinkle the top with cheese and place in the oven on the top rack. Bake until the top is golden brown and bubbly, about 10-12 minutes.

Courtesy of Micqueal's, Glasgow, Kentucky.

Hot Brown

Start with 7 oz. prime beef patty and cooked for desired temperature. Add the following:

3 oz. sliced turkey
3 oz. smoked city ham
2 oz. Mornay cheese sauce
2 slices applewood bacon

Serve on a tomato onion jam compote, plated on your favorite bun. We use buttered brushed brioche bun.

Courtesy of Napa Prime, Versailles, Kentucky.

Italian Beef
(2 days preparation)

1 pc. beef knuckle (choice i.e.; finger) 8-12 lbs.
15 garlic cloves
1 large handful oregano
1 handful kosher salt
1 handful crushed red pepper
1 handful granulated garlic

Rub all of the above into the beef. Put in pan with ½" water and cover and roast at 400 degrees until 140 degree temperature.

Take out and chill overnight. Slice meat as thin as possible against the grain.

Take the drippings and pour into a 1 gallon container. Then divide between 2 gallon containers, and add the rest of the containers with water. Add one tablespoon of all of the above ingredients, with the exception of the red pepper. Just add 1 tsp. of red pepper.

Take sliced meat and put in one of the containers and pour ½ juice over the beef and refrigerate overnight.

Heat the other gallon of au jus as needed for sandwiches. Make sure to stir it up good prior to heating. You can pour juice over French bread for sandwiches or you can dip the sandwich in au jus.

Courtesy of Mugsy's, Murray, Kentucky.

LeeAnn's Ham Casserole

2-3 cups favorite cooked ham cubed or cut into bite size pieces
2-3 cups cooked potatoes, cubed or cut into small pieces (avoid over-cooking)
1 can low sodium and low fat cream of mushroom soup (regular may also be used but will give a saltier taste to casserole)
1 can (soup can) water
1/2-1 cup cubed cheese, Velveeta
1/4 - 1/3 cup shredded mozzarella

Whisk in soup and water together in a glass microwave safe container, then stir in the cubed cheese. Cover with wax paper and cook on high for several minutes depending on the strength of the microwave. I use a small oven and cook for 8 minutes to avoid overcooking, but to ensure cheese melts. This can also be cooked on the stovetop. After cooking, stir well to blend.

Mix ham and potatoes together in baking dish sprayed with cooking spray. Pour Soup/cheese mixture over ham and potatoes and mix well. Mixture should not be too thin or have too much liquid. If it does, add more ham or potatoes. The mix should be about equal.

Bake at 325-350 degrees for 20-30 minutes until hot, bubbly and lightly browned. Remove from oven and sprinkle with shredded mozzarella to taste. Return to oven and bake 5-10 minutes.

Courtesy of Freedom Store Restaurant, Freedom, Kentucky.

Meatloaf

2 lbs. ground chuck
½ cup chopped bell pepper
½ cup chopped onion
1 ½ tsp. garlic powder
2 tsp. salt
1 tsp. black pepper
¼ cup chili powder
2 eggs, beaten
¼ cup catsup

Mix together all ingredients. Form into loaf, place in baking pan. Put catsup on top of loaf.

Bake at 375 degrees for one hour or internal temperature of 165 degrees.

Courtesy of Bub's Café, Elizabethtown, Kentucky.

Parmesan Crusted Mahi-Mahi with Katsu Sauce
(2-8 oz. Mahi-Mahi filets)

Crust
1 cup Parmesan cheese, grated
1/2 cup Panko bread crumbs
2 eggs
1/4 cup whole milk
1 tsp. salt
1 tsp. pepper

In a bowl combine eggs and milk and whisk together. Combine Parmesan cheese, Panko, salt & pepper in separate bowl. Place mahi filets in the egg wash and evenly coat. Coat Mahi with panko mixture, return to egg wash, and coat with panko again. This will give you a good thick crust. Place filet on cookie sheet coated with butter so filets won't stick. Bake at 450 degrees for 10 minutes until golden brown.

Serve on a bed of rice and top with the following:

Katsu Sauce

3 cups water
1 cup catsup
1 cup sugar
½ cup Worcestershire sauce
1 tsp. salt
¼ tsp. white pepper
½ tsp. cornstarch

Combine all ingredients except cornstarch and 1/2 cup water in large saucepan and bring to a boil. Reduce heat to medium and cook for 5 minutes.

Combine cornstarch and 1/2 cup water in a small dish and whisk into sauce mixture. Whisk until consistency desire is reached.

Courtesy of Lizzy B's, Prestonsburg, Kentucky.

Western Omelet

3 eggs, fluffy
Tomatoes
Peppers
Onions
Cheese
Mushrooms
Ham
Bacon
Sausage

Mix all together and pour on grill.
Serve with hashbrowns or home fries, toast or biscuits.

Courtesy of Welch's Riverside Restaurant, Carrollton, Kentucky.

Sides

Buffalo Mac & Cheese

1 Tbl. butter
1 tsp. minced garlic
1 cup cream
2 Tbls. Buffalo sauce
Pinch salt & pepper
3 oz. cooked chicken
¼ cup shredded cheddar
¼ cup shredded provolone
5 oz. cooked penne
1 Tbl. Blue Cheese crumbles

Melt butter in sauté pan. Add garlic, cream, buffalo sauce, salt and pepper, and chicken and reduce.
Add cheese. Be sure to constantly stir to keep cheese from sticking.
Add penne and toss until heated through.
Garnish with blue cheese.
Courtesy of Commonwealth Kitchen & Bar, Henderson, Kentucky.

Corn Pudding

2 lbs. frozen cut corn

Place in a buttered 9" x 11" pan or dish
Mix in a blender:
8 large eggs
1 cup white sugar
1 ½ tsp. seasoned salt
1 ½ tsp. black pepper or Morton's Nature's seasoning blend
1 stick margarine
2-2 ½ cups milk

Make sure mixture is blended thoroughly. Pour over frozen corn and stir to insure it covers all the frozen corn.

Place in a preheated oven at 350 degrees for 55 minutes or until golden
colored.

Courtesy of Parkview Inn, Augusta, Kentucky.

Cornmeal Hoecake

1 cup cornmeal (all purpose)
1 cup self-rising flour
1 tsp. baking powder
½ cup buttermilk
¼ tsp. salt
¼ cup water (as needed)
¼ cup canola oil
3 eggs
½ cup milk
6 Tbl. unsalted butter

In a bowl, whisk together flour, cornmeal, salt and baking powder. Whisk
in buttermilk, water, eggs, butter and oil.
Cook cornmeal hoecakes in cast iron skillet over medium heat about 4-5
inches round making 8-9 cakes.

Courtesy of Longhunters Coffee & Tea Company, Greensburg, Kentucky.

4 large green tomatoes	*2 tsp. paprika*
2 eggs	*¼ tsp. cumin*
2 cups milk	*1 tsp. dried parsley*
2 cups flour	*1 tsp. salt*
4 cups Panko (Japanese bread crumbs)	*1 tsp. pepper*
	1 tsp. chili powder
1 tsp. garlic salt	*½ tsp. cayenne*

Fried Green Tomatoes

Slice tomatoes into 1/4" slices. Mix eggs and milk and set aside. Combine
salt, pepper, and flour and set aside. Combine Panko and the rest of spices.
Dredge tomatoes in flour mixture, then into the milk mixture, then into
the Panko mixture. Press Panko into tomatoes to cover completely.
Fry in vegetable oil at 350 degrees until golden brown. Serve with chow-
chow and ranch.

Courtesy of Otto's, Covington, Kentucky.

Gouda Mac N Cheese

1 box elbow macaroni

Boil to firm tenderness. Drain and rinse it well to stop cooking and to remove starch.

Cheese Sauce
Take half cream and half butter and add Gouda cheese and continue stirring to desired consistency.
Add white pepper and salt to taste.

Pour over macaroni and bake at 350 degrees until browned.
Courtesy of Chandler's, Maysville, Kentucky.

Homemade Dressing

30 slices bread
2 Tbl. butter
1 large onion, finely chopped
2 stalks celery, finely chopped
2 eggs, lightly beaten
2 cups chicken broth
2 tsp. rubbed sage
1 tsp. garlic powder
Salt & pepper

Allow bread to sit out overnight until hard.
Pre-heat oven to 325 degrees.
Crush bread into crumbs with a rolling pin and put crumbs into a large bowl.
Melt butter in medium saucepan over medium heat. Stir in onion and celery and cook slowly until soft. Remove from heat and drain.

Mix the eggs and chicken broth into the breadcrumbs. The mixture should be moist, but not mushy. Then add onion, celery, sage, garlic powder, salt and pepper.
Pour mixture into baking pan. Bake for one hour until the top is brown and crisp.
Courtesy of Hardscratch Country Store, Columbia, Kentucky.

Pimento Cheese

1 cup shredded cheese
½ cup apple cider vinegar
1 ¼ cup Miracle Whip
1 ¼ cup sugar
1 can pimentos
1 block Velveeta cheese

Mix shredded cheese, vinegar, mayo, sugar and pimentos on medium speed for 3-5 minutes.
Add chunks of Velveeta cheese while the mixer is still on. Mix on medium to high speed for 5 minutes.

Courtesy of Chaney's Dairy Barn, Bowling Green, Kentucky.

Sweet Potato Casserole

1 large can sweet potatos
1 cup sugar
2 eggs
½ cup milk
½ tsp. salt
1/3 stick melted margarine
1 tsp. vanilla

Mix well and pour into buttered pan.

Topping
1 cup brown sugar
½ cup all-purpose flour
1 cup crushed pecans
1/3 cup melted margarine
Mix and sprinkle on top of casserole
Bake 35 to 45 minutes on 350 degrees.

Courtesy of Anchor Grill, Covington, Kentucky.

Stewed Tomatoes

1 stick butter
½ cup diced onions
½ cup green peppers
4 chicken bouillon cubes
Nature's Blend & Seasoned Salt Herb & Garlic
¼ cup sugar
4 heaping Tbl. brown sugar
1 cup water
7 slices bread (sourdough)

Sauté onion & peppers in butter until tender. Add bouillon cubes & seasonings. Add diced tomatoes & rinse can with water. Add sugar. Bring to a boil, simmer 10 minutes, add bread cubes and turn off heat.

Courtesy of Parkview Inn, Augusta, Kentucky.

Desserts

Apple Cake with Custard Glaze

3 cups flour
2 tsp. baking powder
1/8 tsp. salt
¼ tsp. ground cloves
¼ tsp. ground nutmeg
6 oz. softened butter

¾ cup sugar
4 large apples
2 eggs
¾ cup milk
2 tsp. sugar (to sprinkle on cake)

Pre-heat oven to 375 degrees.

Grease and flour an 8" or 9" round spring-form pan. Sift flour, baking powder, salt, cloves and nutmeg in a large mixing bowl. Cut butter into flour mixture until it resembles fine crumbs. Add ¾ cup sugar to flour mixture and mix in.

Peel and cut apples into chunks and toss into mixture.

In separate bowl, beat eggs and milk together. Add to dry mixture until just combined. Batter will be thick.

Transfer dough into pan and flatten surface. Sprinkle sugar over top of dough.

Bake 45-50 minutes until golden and knife comes out clean.

Custard
(will be thin and sauce-like)
6 eggs
6 Tbl. sugar
1 ½ cups milk, hot
1 ½ tsp. vanilla

Place egg yolks and sugar in a bowl and whisk until pale, 2-3 minutes.

Place milk in saucepan and bring just to a boil.

Slowly whisk hot milk into egg mixture. Transfer back to saucepan over medium heat until slightly thickened, about 4 minutes until custard coats back of a spoon.

Serve cake warm with custard glaze.

Courtesy of Cobbler's Café, Elizabethtown, Kentucky.

Banana Pudding

5 cups milk, scalded
6 egg yolks, beaten well
1 ½ cup sugar
2/3 cup cornstarch
pinch - Salt
6-7 bananas
1 ½ boxes vanilla wafers
2 Tbl. butter
2 tsp. vanilla

Mix sugar, cornstarch, and salt in bowl. Heat milk until a film comes over top. Add dry mix, stir constantly.

Add in beaten egg yolks slowly, continue to stir. Remove from heat when it starts to thicken. Add butter and vanilla.

Layer vanilla wafers, pudding and bananas in baking dish.

Meringue
8 egg whites
1 cup sugar
Pinch cornstarch
2 tsp. vanilla

Beat egg whites and vanilla on high. As it gets frothy gradually add sugar and cornstarch mix. Beat until stiff. Put on top of pudding. Bake at 400 degrees for 5-7 minutes. Remove. Take a few vanilla wafers and crumble on top.

Courtesy of Brook's, Sonora, Kentucky.

Banana Split Cake

1 scoop of flour
2 handfuls of brown sugar
2 handfuls of pecans
Melted butter

Mix above until crumbly. Bake at 350 degrees until golden brown. Set aside and cool.

¼ stick of butter
3 eggs
2 lbs. powdered sugar

Mix above and pour over cooled crust.

3 bananas, sliced
1 can crushed pineapple
1 tub cool whip
Crushed pecans

Slice bananas on top of filling, add crushed pineapple and top with Cool
Whip and crushed pecans.

Courtesy of Rosie's, Olive Hill, Kentucky.

Blueberry Crumb Cake

½ lb. unsalted butter, softened
1 1/3 c. granulated sugar
4 large eggs
1 ½ tsp. baking powder
1 tsp. salt
2 cups All-purpose flour

Topping
2 cups All-purpose flour
1 cup brown sugar
1 ½ tsp. cinnamon
½ lb. unsalted butter, softened

3 cups blueberries, fresh or frozen (can use other fruit – peaches, raspberries,
and apples all work well)

Preparation
Make the topping: In a food processor, combine the topping ingredients
(flour, brown sugar, butter and cinnamon). Pulse the motor until
topping is combined well and crumbly. This step can also be done by
hand with a pastry cutter or fork.
Preheat the oven to 350° and grease a 9" x 13" or 10" square baking pan.
With an electric mixer, cream the butter and the granulated sugar

until light and fluffy. Add eggs one at a time, beating well after each addition. Mix together the flour, baking powder, and salt and add to the egg-butter-sugar mixture. Blend the batter until it is just combined (it will be very thick).

Spread ½ of the batter in the prepared pan. Sprinkle on ½ of the fruit, then ½ of the topping. Repeat the layers of batter, fruit and topping with remaining ingredients. Bake the cake in the middle of the oven for 50 minutes – 1 hour or until tester comes out clean. Serve cake warm or at room temperature.

Courtesy of Q&A Sweet Treats, LaGrange, Kentucky.

Bread Pudding

8 hamburger buns, cut in cubes or 1 loaf French bread, cubed
4 eggs, beaten
4 cups milk, scalded
1 ½ cup sugar
½ stick melted butter
¼ tsp. nutmeg
¼ tsp. salt

Butter a 9x13x2 inch-baking dish. Place bread crumbs in dish.
Beat eggs and sugar until lemon colored.
Scald milk just until bubbly; do not over boil. Stir in egg and sugar mixture; add salt and butter. Stir in nutmeg.
Pour over cubed bread. Bake in 350-degree oven for 30-35 minutes. Remove from oven and cool.
Pour nutmeg sauce over pudding. Serve with dollop of either whipped topping or whipped cream.
Serve with rum sauce.

Rum Sauce
¾ cup sugar
1 Tbl. cornstarch
2/3 cup water
1/3 cup rum
½ tsp. lemon juice
1 Tbl. butter or margarine

Combine first four ingredients in a small saucepan. Bring to a boil over medium heat.

Cook 1 minute, stirring constantly. Add lemon juice and butter.
Stir until butter melts. Serve warm. Yield: 1 ½ cups.

Courtesy of Catfish Kitchen, Draffenville, Kentucky.

Bread Pudding

2 cups sugar
3 eggs
1 Tbl. vanilla
¼ cup butter
2 cups milk
9 crumbled biscuits

Mix together sugar, eggs, vanilla, butter and milk. Add crumbled
  biscuits.
Put in greased 9 x 13 pan and bake 40 minutes at 350 degrees.

Topping
1 cup sugar
1 cup water
2 Tbls. cornstarch
1 tsp. vanilla
2 Tbls. butter

Bring to a boil stirring constantly. Remove from heat.
Add 2 Tbls. butter and 1 tsp. vanilla. Mix and spread on top of baked
  pudding.

Courtesy of KayLee's Farmhouse Restaurant, Aurora, Kentucky.

Buckeye Brownies

1 box fudge brownies
2 cups powdered sugar
½ cup unsalted butter, softened
8 Tbl. Unsalted butter, softened
1 cup creamy peanut butter
1 cup milk chocolate chips

In a 9" x 12" pan, make and bake brownies and let cool.
In a bowl add powdered sugar, ½ cup butter and peanut butter. Mix well
  and spread over top of your brownies.

Melt together chocolate chips and remaining butter in a saucepan over medium heat until all melted, then pour over top of peanut butter and refrigerate for an hour.

Then serve and enjoy!

Courtesy of Jane's Saddlebag, Union, Kentucky.

Buttermilk Pie

1 cup buttermilk
2 cups sugar
3 eggs
4 Tbl. butter
2 Tbl. flour
1 tsp. vanilla

Mix all ingredients and pour into 9" pie shell. Bake at 350 degrees for one hour.

Courtesy of Bub's Café, Elizabethtown, Kentucky.

Chess Pie
(2 pies)

6 eggs
4 cups sugar
¼ cup cornmeal
1 cup evaporated milk
1 cup melted butter or margarine

Mix well. Pour into two – 10" unbaked pie shells.
Bake at 350 degrees for 1 hour or until set and golden brown.

Courtesy of Dixie Pan Restaurant, Nortonville, Kentucky.

Chocolate or Coconut Pie

For chocolate pie:
1 ½ cups sugar
4 Tbls. Cocoa
3 cups milk (1 ½ regular and 1 ½ evaporated)
¼ cup flour

4 egg yolks
1 tsp. vanilla
1 stick butter

Cook the above ingredients for 15 minutes in microwave and add 1 stick of butter and mix well. Top with meringue.

Coconut Pie

All of the above ingredients without the cocoa. Top with meringue.

Meringue
4 egg whites
½ cup sugar

Beat until peaks form and bake at 350 degrees until top of peaks golden brown.

Courtesy of Short's Family Restaurant, Graham, Kentucky.

German Chocolate Pie

1 cup sugar
1 Tbl. cornstarch
2 Tbl. cocoa
2 Tbl. flour
¼ tsp. salt

Mix above ingredients together. Then add:

2/3 cup milk
3 Tbl. melted butter
2 eggs, beaten
1 Tbl. vanilla
½ cup chopped pecans
1 cup shredded coconut
1-9" pie crust

Mix all ingredients well and pour into an unbaked pie crust. Bake at 350 degrees for 40 minutes.

Courtesy of Fava's, Georgetown, Kentucky.

Macaroon Haystacks

8 cups shredded snowflake coconut
2 cups granulated sugar (fine)
1 cup egg whites (6-8 eggs)
1 tsp. vanilla extract

In large bowl toss the coconut and sugar. Then add the egg whites and vanilla
and mix with your hands until all combined well. (It will be sticky).
Use a large cookie scoop to make even cookie mounds on parchment
paper. Cool at 350 degrees for 12-15 minutes until browned. They will
be crunchy on the outside and gooey on the inside.

Courtesy of Boyce General Store, Alvaton, Kentucky.

Peach Bread Pudding

1 dozen jumbo hamburger buns, shredded
18 eggs
4 cups heavy whipping cream
4 cups milk
2 Tbl. cinnamon
1 tsp. vanilla
2 cups brown sugar
1 cup sugar
1 #10 can peaches

Blend all ingredients together and drain for excess liquid. Place mixture
into 11.5" x 9.25" aluminum baking pan.
Bake at 400 degrees until top is golden brown approximately 30 minutes.

Courtesy of Red State BBQ, Lexington, Kentucky.

Persimmon Cookies

½ cup shortening
½ cup brown sugar
½ cup white sugar
1 cup persimmon pulp
1 egg
2 cups sifted flour

½ tsp. nutmeg
½ tsp. salt
1 tsp. cinnamon
1 cup nuts
1 cup dates or raisins (chopped)
1 tsp. vanilla

Cream together shortening, sugars, persimmon pulp and egg. Sift together
   remaining dry ingredients and add to creamed mixture. Add nuts,
   dates and vanilla.

Drop from tsp. onto greased cookie sheet. Bake in 350 degree oven about
   20 minutes.

If desired, use a few red candy hearts melted, or more cinnamon instead
   of nutmeg.

Courtesy of Lite Side Bakery & Deli, Grand Rivers, Kentucky.

Fresh Strawberry Pie

2 Tbl. melted butter
1 Tbl. sugar
9 inch short crust pie shell, baked
Fresh whole strawberries, enough to fill the crust

Pat short crust into a 9-inch tart pan with removable bottom. Bake
at 375 degrees, approximately 7-10 minutes until lightly browned.
While crust is hot from the oven, sprinkle it with melted butter and
sugar. Set aside to cool.

Strawberry Glaze

1 cup sugar or honey
1 Tbl. cornstarch
1 Tbl. red wine vinegar
1 Tbl. butter
½ cup water
2 cups strawberries (measure before crushing)

Crush berries in food processor. Mix with remaining ingredients. Cook
   and stir over medium heat until clear, about 5 minutes. Let cool.

Fill crust with whole berries and pour glaze over fruit. Chill and serve.

Short Crust

1 ¼ cups All-purpose Flour
¼ tsp. salt
7 Tbl. butter
Water

Combine all ingredients in food processor. Pulse and add enough water until it begins to stick together. With floured hands, press into a 9-inch pie pan.

Courtesy of Snug Hollow, Irvine, Kentucky.

Tea Bayou Beignets

A twist on a New Orleans favorite, our beignets has a vanilla-lemon bite that brightens the flavor of the dough.

½ oz. yeast
1 ½ cup warm water (105 degrees)
½ cup granulated sugar
1 tsp. salt
2 eggs, beaten
1 cup milk
2 tsp. lemon extract
1 tsp. vanilla extract
7 cups all-purpose flour
¼ cup butter, softened
Oil for frying
Powdered sugar

In electric mixer bowl, dissolve yeast in warm water; let stand five minutes. On low, beat sugar, salt, eggs and milk into yeast mixture; add lemon and vanilla. On low, beat in half of the flour, then butter, and blend until smooth. Gradually add remaining flour, and blend until well incorporated. Cover with plastic wrap and chill at least 4 hours.

Fill large pot with oil to the depth of at least 3". Preheat oil to 305 degrees (important that the oil is at temperature before frying). Roll dough onto floured board to 1/8" thickness; cut into 3" squares.

Drop a couple of beignets into oil (do not crowd them). Fry until puffy and light brown (2-3 minutes each side). Drain well on paper towels. Sift a generous amount of powdered sugar on top of hot beignets and serve immediately.

Courtesy of Tea Bayou, Bowling Green, Kentucky.

About the Author

Gary P. West has simple criteria when it comes to writing books.

"I only take on a project that I will enjoy writing about and I only write about something I think people will enjoy reading," he says.

West grew up in Elizabethtown, Kentucky and attended Western Kentucky University before graduating from the University of Kentucky in 1967 with a journalism degree. At U.K. he was a daily sports editor for the Kentucky Kernel.

Later he served as editor for the nation's largest civilian enterprise military newspaper at Fort Bragg, North Carolina. From there he was employed in the corporate advertising office of one of the country's largest insurance companies, State Farm Insurance in Bloomington, Illinois, where he was a copywriter.

He returned to Kentucky in 1972 where he began an advertising and publishing business.

Along the way, for twelve years, he was the executive director of the Hilltopper Athletic Foundation at Western Kentucky University, and provided color commentary for Wes Strader on the Hilltopper Basketball Network.

In 1993, he became the executive director of the Bowling Green Area Convention and Visitors Bureau. He retired from there in 2006 to devote more time to his writing.

He is a freelance writer for several magazines in addition to writing a syndicated newspaper travel column, *Out & About...Kentucky Style*, for several papers across the state.

Gary is in demand as a speaker and for book signings throughout Kentucky.

This is his ninth book. Previous books are *King Kelley Coleman: Kentucky's Greatest Basketball Legend* (2005), *Eating Your Way Across Kentucky* (2006), *Eating Your Way Across Kentucky – The Recipes* (2007), *Shopping Your Way Across Kentucky* (2009), *101 Must Places to Visit in Kentucky Before You Die* (2009), *The Boys From Corbin: America's Greatest Little Sports Town* (2013), and co-authored *Kentucky Colonels of the American Basketball Association: The Real Story of a Team Left Behind* (2011) and *Better Than Gold: Olympian Kenny Davis and the Most Controversial Basketball Game in History* (2014).

Gary and his wife, Deborah, live in Bowling Green, Kentucky.

Gary and Deborah West pose for the cover photo at the 1930s replica service station owned by Rik and Sandy Hawkins. The photographer is David Toczko.

INDEX

A

Ahlschwede, Scott 108
Alexiou, Dino 198
Alvaton, Kentucky 122, 130, 250
Andriot, Bob 58
Andriot, Sue 58
Augusta, Kentucky 160, 182, 239, 242
Aurora, Kentucky 12, 34, 247

B

Bailey, Shirley 66
Ballou, Jimmy 135
Bardstown, Kentucky 56, 94
Baron, Jay 44, 45
Baron, Maria 44
Bedford, Kentucky 160, 174
Benton, Kentucky 12, 26, 46, 225
Berea, Kentucky 186, 198
Bernheim Forest 80
Bernheim, Isaac 80
Bird, Rodger 201
Blackmore, Brett 168, 169
Blackmore, Nancy 168
Blackmore, Peter 168
Blackmore, Samantha 168
Bowen, John 90
Bowen, Kaylyn 90
Bowen, Michelle 90
Bowling, Alice 76
Bowling Green, Kentucky 122, 132, 158, 241, 252
Bragg, Lee Ann 140
Bragg, Willard 140
Brandenburg, Kentucky 56, 82

Branham, Tim 206, 207
Brooks, Ella Mae 64
Brooks, Robert 64
Bruen, Margaret 192
Bryan, Bob 40
Bryan, Irene 40
Burden, Jayme 74
Burke, Joe 69
Burke, Patty 69
Burkesville, Kentucky 122, 124, 225
Burlington, Kentucky 160, 182
Burnside, Kentucky 122, 146, 227

C

Cadiz, Kentucky 12, 38, 48
Caffrey, Mike 210
Carpenter, Brian 210
Carroll, David 108
Carrollton, Kentucky 160, 184, 237
Carson, Johnny 36
Cartwright, Christina 21
Chaney, Carl 132, 133
Chaney, Debra 132
Chapman, Carolyn 162, 163
Clark, Christy 94
Clark, Daniel 94
Clark, Robyn 94
Clay, Elizabeth 72, 73
Clay, Frank 72
Clay, Henry 72
Clermont, Kentucky 56, 80
Coe, Geneva 136
Coe, George 136
Coe, Gerald 136
Columbia, Kentucky 122, 148, 240

Copelin, Delores 64
Copelin, Rhonda 64
Corbin, Kentucky 186, 200
Corbin, Matt 190
Correll, Angela 60
Correll, Jess 60
Covington, Kentucky 160,
162, 176, 239, 241
Cox, Sheila 66
Cynthiana, Kentucky 160,
172

D

Danville, Kentucky 56, 62,
68
Davis, Judy 16
Davis, Kenny 134, 135
Davis, Wes 16
DeMatteo, Tony 168
Draffenville, Kentucky 12,
16, 247
Duggin, Jim 137

E

Elizabethtown, Kentucky
56, 66, 74, 236, 243,
248
Erlanger, Kentucky 160,
166, 222
Erskine, John 156
Erskine, Sebrina 156
Essenpries, Andrea 104
Exler, Linda 167

F

Fairdale, Kentucky 57,
112, 228
Fava, Louie 78
Fava, Susie Bertolini 78
Flay, Bobby 60
Flynn, Mary Lou 34, 35
Frankfort, Kentucky 56,
100
Franklin, Kentucky 122,
142

Frederick, Peggy 76, 77
Frederick, Randy 76, 77
Frederick, Robert 76, 77
Frederick, Scott 76, 77
Freedom, Kentucky 122,
140, 236

G

Gant, Donny 142
Gant, Wendy 142
Gardner, Lloyd 112
Garr, Carolyn 200
Garr, Ed 200
Garrett, Jessie 20
Georgetown, Kentucky 56,
78, 249
Gilbertsville, Kentucky 12,
38
Glasgow, Kentucky 122,
154, 234
Goldman, Barb 178, 181
Golliher, Brad 130, 131
Golliher, Brie 130, 131
Graham, Kentucky 12, 52,
249
Grand Rivers, Kentucky
12, 40, 251
Grant, Susan 203
Grant, Thomas 203
Green, Erika 84, 85
Greensburg, Kentucky 56,
92, 239
Grimes, Matt 166, 167
Grimes, Noelle 166
Gruchow, John 78
Guthrie, Angelique 146
Guthrie, William 146

H

Hannan, David 124, 125
Hannan, Heather 124, 125
Harden, Nancy 138
Hardin, Kentucky 12, 38
Harrodsburg, Kentucky 56,
102

Hawkins, Bill 60
Hawkins, Rik 256
Hawkins, Sandy 256
Hazard, Kentucky 186,
    218, 231
Hazel, Kentucky 12, 14,
    226
Helton, Mike 192
Helton, Pam 192
Henderson, Kentucky 12,
    18, 50, 238
Hines, Duncan 8
Hirsch, Deborah 126, 127
Hirsch, Richard 126
Hodgenville, Kentucky 56,
    88
Holliday, Harry 26
Hooper, Martha 26
Hopkinsville, Kentucky 12,
    24
Howard, Justin 150
Howard, Rebecca 150, 151
Hughes, Bill 174, 175

I

Independence, Kentucky
    232
Irvine, Kentucky 186, 216,
    252
Island, Kentucky 12, 22

J

James, Frank 83
James, Jesse 83
Jamestown, Kentucky 122,
    152

K

Keen, Ron 150
Kelder, Pete 86
Kelley, Sherri 148
Kelley, Tim 148
Kirk-Dillow, Kasey 42
Kirk, Jenne 42
Kirk, Larry 42

Knoth, Frances 36
Knoth, Hugh 36
Knoth, Leonard 36

L

LaGrange, Kentucky 57,
    104, 106, 246
Laha, Anita 88, 89
Laha, Ethan 89
Laha, Kelly 89
Laha, Sally 88
Laha, William 88
Lake City, Kentucky 12, 36
Landrum, Bill 92, 93
Landrum, Justine 92
Leno, Jay 36
Lewis, Darrell 98
Lewis, Lori 98
Lexington, Kentucky 56,
    57, 86, 108, 118, 223,
    250
Lindsey, Bobby 144
Lindsey, Teresa 144, 145
Logan, Mark 18
London, Kentucky 186,
    210
Louisville, Kentucky 56,
    57, 70, 76, 96, 120

M

Madisonville, Kentucky 12,
    20, 224
Masters, Colin 62
Mathis, Gloria 17
Matthews, Michael 154,
    155
Maysville, Kentucky 160,
    164, 178, 224, 240
McReynolds, Jackson 118
Meadors, Bill "Yogi" 201
Midgett, Debbie 80, 81
Miller, Mary 58
Miller, Shirley 52
Monticello, Kentucky 122,
    134

Morehead, Eric 182
Morehead, Kentucky 186, 202, 230
Morgan, John Hunt 83
Morgantown, Kentucky 122, 144
Munoz, Jayson 18, 19
Murphy, Claude 112
Murphy, Lennie 112
Murray, Kentucky 12, 44, 54, 226, 235
Murrow, Cheri 70
Murrow, Joe 70
Murrow, John 70, 71
Murrow, Mary 70
Murrow, Tom 70
Muse, Karen 54
Mylor, Justin 170, 171
Mylor, Rena 170, 171

N

Nance, Cliff 20
Nancy, Kentucky 122, 138, 139, 233
Napier, Barbara 216
Noble, Jenn 218
Nortonville, Kentucky 12, 28, 248

O

Olive Hill, Kentucky 186, 196, 245
Overstreet, Anita 83
Owensboro, Kentucky 12, 42, 228

P

Paducah, Kentucky 12, 30, 32, 233
Paintsville, Kentucky 186, 194
Palombino, Judy 96, 97
Palombino, Tony 96, 97
Paris, Kentucky 56, 72, 233

Parsons, Don 114
Paschall, Barb 14, 15
Paschall, Scooter 14
Payneville, Kentucky 57, 116
Pendergest, Joe 84, 85
Pikeville, Kentucky 186, 188, 190, 224
Poff, Lisa 137
Powell, Nancy 128
Presley, John 100, 101
Prestonsburg, Kentucky 186, 204, 206, 237
Prowse, Jerry 28
Prowse, Ruth Ann 28, 29
Purdy, Kristen 212
Purdy, Robert 212

R

Radar, Rick 110
Ravencraft, David Lowe 118
Rice, Jenny 182
Richardson, Darold 90
Richardson, Olene 90
Richmond, Kentucky 186, 212
Robinson, Missy 163
Rush, Kentucky 186, 214
Russell Springs, Kentucky 122, 136, 232
Russellville, Kentucky 122, 126, 128, 227

S

Samuels, Michael 134
Schmidt, Ella 137
Scott, Brad 118
Scottsville, Kentucky 122, 150, 156
Selby, Tony 108
Shea, Greg 158, 159
Shea, Theresa 158, 159
Shelbyville, Kentucky 56, 58

Short, Bobby 52
Short, Paula 52
Signa, Paul 30
Simpsonville, Kentucky 56,
    84
Sivells, Barbara 112
Sivells, Mike 112, 113
Skorpil, Alexandra 24
Skorpil, Pavel 24, 25
Slade, Kentucky 186, 208
Slayden, Daniel 46
Sonora, Kentucky 56, 64,
    244
Stanford, Kentucky 56, 60
Stanton, Kentucky 186,
    192
Stephensburg, Kentucky
    56, 90
Stewart, Marty 137
Stull, Marlinda 116

T
Taylor, Don 22
Taylor, Henry 22, 23
Taylor, Lydia 22
Taylor, Owsley 22
Taylor, Tim 22
Thomas, Dan 203
Thomas, Fred 51
Thomas, Marge 203
Thomas, Mary Beth 172
Thomas, Rodney 50
Tierney, John 196
Toczko, David 256
Troutman, Ellie 106

U
Union, Kentucky 160, 168,
    248

V
Ventura, Dario 208
Ventura, Miguel 208, 209
Ventura, Susan 208, 209
Versailles, Kentucky 56,
    57, 98, 110, 229, 234

W
Wagner, Brenda 121
Wagner, Karen 121
Wagner, Lee 121
Wainscott, Brad 182
Warner, Chan 164
Warsaw, Kentucky 160,
    170
Weckman, Paul 176, 177
Welch, Donna 184
Welch, Tammy 184
West, Deborah 255, 256
Westfall, Josh 110
White, Anita 32
White, Ken 32, 33
White, Lora 102
Wilkinson, Wallace 136
Williams, Hank, Jr. 137
Williams, Hank, Sr. 83
Winchester, Kentucky 57,
    74, 114, 222

Y
Yokley, Mary 142
Yokley, Willis 142

RESTAURANT INDEX

A

Anchor Grill 160, 162, 241
Angelo's Family Restaurant
& Bar 232
Annie Ruby's Café 122,
124, 225
Ariella Bistro & Bar 122,
126, 227

B

Bank 247 186, 188
Bell House Restaurant 56,
58
Bethel Dipper 122, 128
Bluebird Café 56, 60
Bluegrass Pizza 56, 62
Blue Raven 186, 190, 224
Blue & White Grill 12, 14,
226
Boyce General Store 122,
130, 250
Brook's General Store Café
56, 64, 244
Bruen's Restaurant 186,
192
Bub's Café 56, 66, 236,
248
Burke's Bakery 56, 68

C

Carriage House Restaurant
186, 194
Carter Cave State Park
186, 196
Catfish Kitchen 12, 16, 247
Chandler's Restaurant &
Bar 160, 164, 240
Chaney's Dairy Barn 122,
132, 241
Check's 56, 70
City Pool Hall 122, 134

Clay's Downtown 56, 72,
233
Cobbler's Café 56, 74, 243
Coe's Restaurant 122,
136, 232
Colonial Cottage Inn 160,
166, 222
Commonwealth Kitchen &
Bar 12, 18, 238
Corner Café 56, 76
Crowded House, The 12,
20, 224

D

Dairy Freeze 12, 22
DaVinci's Little Italian Res-
taurant 12, 24
Dinner Bell 12, 26
Dino's Italian Restaurant
186, 198
Dixie Café 186, 200
Dixie Pan Restaurant 12,
28, 248
Doe's Eat Place 12, 30,
233

F

Fava's Restaurant 56, 78,
249
Fishtales 122, 138, 233
Freedom Store & Restau-
rant 122, 140, 236
Frosty Freeze 122, 142
Fuzzy Duck Café 186,
202, 230

G

Gold Rush Café 12, 32
Gone Fishin' 122, 144
Guthrie's River House 122,
146, 227

263

H

Hardscratch Country Store 122, 148, 240
Hickory Hill BBQ 122, 150

I

Isaac's Café 56, 80

J

Jailhouse Pizza 56, 82
Jane's Saddlebag 160, 168, 248
Jenny Wiley State Park 186, 204
Jewell's On Main 160, 170
JT's Pizza & Subs 56, 84

K

KayLee's Farmhouse Restaurant 12, 34, 247
Keeneland Track Kitchen 56, 86
Kenlake 12
Kenlake - Aurora Landing Restaurant 38
Kentucky Dam Village 12
Kentucky Dam Village - Harbor Lights Restaurant 38
Knoth's BarBQue 12, 36

L

Laha's Red Castle 56, 88
Lake Barkley 12
Lake Barkley, Kenlake, Kentucky Dam Village 38
Lake Barkley - Window on the Water Dining Room 38
Lake Cumberland State Resort Park 122, 152
Laker Drive-In 56, 90
Leono's 160, 172
Lite Side Café & Bakery 12, 40, 251

Little Town & Country Restaurant 160, 174
Lizzie B's Café 186, 206, 237
Longhunters Coffee & Tea Company 56, 92, 239

M

Mammy's 56, 94
Manny & Merle 56, 96
Margie's Southern Café 224
Micqueal's Bistro 122, 154, 234
Miguel's Pizza 186, 208
Miller House 12, 42, 228
Mugsy's Hideout 12, 44, 235

N

Napa Prime 56, 98, 234

O

Office Pub & Deli 56, 100
Olde Bus Station 56, 102
Old Town Grill 186, 210
Otto's 160, 176, 239

P

Paradise Point 122, 156
Parc Café 160, 178
Parcell's Deli & Grill 12, 46, 225
Parkview Country Inn 160, 180, 239, 242
Purdy's Coffee Company 186, 212

Q

Q & A Sweet Treats 57, 104, 246

R

Rails Restaurant & Bar 57, 106

Red State BBQ 57, 108, 250

Reva's Place 12, 48

Ricardo's Grill & Pub 57, 110, 229

Rookies Food & Spirits 12, 50

Rosie's Restaurant 186, 214, 245

S

Shack in the Back BBQ 57, 112, 228

Short's Family Restaurant 12, 52, 249

Snug Hollow 186, 216, 252

Stinky and Coco's 57, 114, 222

Stull's Country Store 57, 116

Suggins Bar & Grill 57, 118, 223

T

Tea Bayou 122, 158, 252

Tousey House 160, 182

Tree House Café & Bakery 186, 218, 231

W

Wagner's Pharmacy 57, 120

Welch's Riverside Restaurant 160, 184, 237

Wild Mountain Bakery & Café 12, 54, 226

RECIPE INDEX

Soups, Salads & Starters
Beef Barley Soup 222
Coleslaw 222
Fried Banana Peppers 222
Goat Cheese Salad with Honey Pistachio Vinaigrette 223
Gumbo 224
Lettuce Wraps 224
Summer Salad 225
Taco Soup 225
Tomato Basil Soup 226
Vinegar Slaw 226

Sauces & Dressings
Bleu Cheese Dressing 227
Bourbon Alfredo Sauce 227
Bourbon Blueberry Sauce 227
Champagne Honey Vinaigrette Salad Dressing 228
White Lightnin' Sauce 228

Drinks
Caramel Mocha Jo 230
Sleigh Ride 230

Main Dishes
Autumn Sandwich, The 231
Baked Tenderloin 231
Beef Tips/Noodles 232
Chili 232
Crab Cakes 233
Fish Tacos 233
Grilled Chicken Pasta Bake with Mornay Sauce 234
Hot Brown 234
Italian Beef 235
LeeAnn's Ham Casserole 235
Meatloaf 236
Parmesan Crusted Mahi-Mahi with Katsu Sauce 236
Western Omelet 237

Sides
Buffalo Mac & Cheese 238
Cornmeal Hoecake 239
Corn Pudding 238
Fried Green Tomatoes 239
Gouda Mac N Cheese 240
Homemade Dressing 240
Pimento Cheese 241
Stewed Tomatoes 242
Sweet Potato Casserole 241

Desserts
Apple Cake with Custard Glaze 243
Banana Pudding 244
Banana Split Cake 244
Blueberry Crumb Cake 245
Bread Pudding 246, 247
Buckeye Brownies 247
Buttermilk Pie 248
Chess Pie 248
Chocolate Pie 248
Coconut Pie 249
Fresh Strawberry Pie 251
German Chocolate Pie 249
Macaroon Haystacks 250
Peach Bread Pudding 250
Persimmon Cookies 250
Tea Bayou Beignets 252

Other books by Gary P. West
WWW.ACCLAIMPRESS.COM

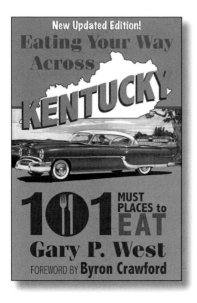

There are literally thousands of eating places in Kentucky. Some are outstanding, some good, some fair and some not so good. It seems it would be easy to identify "101 must places to eat" in the state, but it is a much more daunting task than one would think. What author Gary West has done in these pages is to select eateries that in all probability you may not even know about. Oh sure, the locals eat there and know they are great, but some of the restaurants are not well known to outsiders - until now!

The criteria for making the 101 is simple: it cannot be a chain restaurant and, except for a rare exception, must have been in operation for at least five years. And, of course, the food must be exceptionally delicious!

Beautifully illustrated with detailed directions and menu reviews, this book is guaranteed to thrill the traveler trekking across the bluegrass in his never-ending pursuit of his next dining delight.

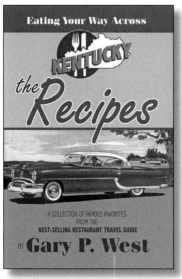

Now, there is no excuse for not serving tasty meals at home. With this book you get the best of both worlds. Not only does it let you know where *101 Must Places To Eat* are located, it now gives you their recipes. For the most part this is not about gourmet food, although some recipes might be considered that. If you are expecting recipes that are all about simple food, this is your book! Cooking in Kentucky is all about simple food! These recipes have been created years ago, usually handed down within families from generation to generation. In a few cases recipes were based on taste, "*I don't measure anything,*" said one restaurant owner. "*I have done it so long I just know what amount to put in.*" When it's all said and done, it is indeed about the taste, regardless of how the cook or chef got there. A measured pour of this and a pinch of that only matters when the end result is a delicious meal that you can now prepare in your own kitchen. Hopefully, this will hold you over until you can get back to the little restaurant from which it came.

Based on last year's best selling *Eating Your Way Across Kentucky-101 Must Places to Eat*, Gary West's sequel *Eating Your Way Across Kentucky-The Recipes* picks and tells the best recipes from choice restaurants. Provides brief description of chefs & owners. Gives complete recipe with ingredients and special techniques for these most famous dishes.

The criteria for making the 101 are that it cannot be a chain restaurant, and, except for a rare exception, must have been in operation for at least five years. And, of course, the food must be exceptionally delicious.

Beautifully illustrated with detailed directions and menu reviews, this book is guaranteed to thrill the traveler trekking across the bluegrass in his never-ending pursuit of his next dining delight.

Anything you could ever want or need can be found right here in the Bluegrass State! In his third installment of things to do all over Kentucky, author Gary West visits some of the most interesting stores in the state – places to shop, that is.

Shopping Your Way Across Kentucky features 101 of the best places to shop in the Commonwealth, from furniture to clothing, knick-knacks to jewelry, and everything in between. The majority of the featured shops are privately owned, with some state shops — no chain stores — many of which have been in business for decades because of the quality of what they sell and their focus on customer service.

In an age where people shop "online" for convenience, Gary's book brings back the pleasure of spending the day strolling through the aisles of one's favorite store – and the stores featured here are ones you won't want to miss!

In his introduction, Gary states, "The thought here is that shopping should be combined with an enjoyable meal, and if traveling overnight, comfortable lodging. It's the total package that makes for a memorable experience."

When you visit these 101 shops, tell 'em that Gary sent 'ya.

Over the past several years some of my friends have said they would like to do what I'm doing: writing books about interesting places to eat and fun places to shop. I've replied with the much overused phrase, but appropriate, that "somebody had to do it."

Criss-crossing the state, visiting almost all of Kentucky's 120 counties, I have assembled *101 Must Places To Visit in Kentucky Before You Die*. These "Must Places" are probably just down the road from where you live. Some are well-known attractions, others not so much. Some cost to see, while some are free. Regardless, all are worth a visit.

A book listing 101 must places to visit is a huge undertaking. However, in the end it confirms an inventory of some of the best-known and unknown places in Kentucky.

Some are historical, some entertaining, others outright fun, while a few are whimsical or even quirky. You can be sure that in these pages there is something for everyone.

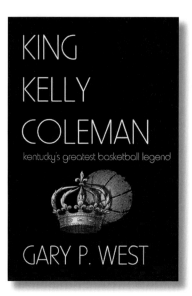

In a state where the love of basketball itself is legendary, there are its rare heroes who also, through the dispassionate lens of history, rise to legendary status. When that legend rises so far above the others as to acquire mythical or rather, folk hero, proportions - and then enigmatically vanishes- you have King Kelly Coleman.

This shy, humble mountain boy blessed with extraordinary talent and drive captured Kentucky's hearts and its all-time record books with performances that have yet to be equaled – even half a century later. Never before in print, the authorized King Kelly Coleman story, is told by award-winning author Gary P. West, from actual interviews and information from Coleman himself.

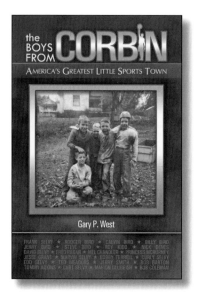

What do the Los Angeles Lakers, St. Louis Cardinals, New York Knicks, San Diego Chargers, Oakland Raiders, Kentucky Wildcats, Louisville Cardinals, Western Kentucky Hilltoppers, Furman Paladins and the Eastern Kentucky Colonels all have in common? They have all had star athletes who began their careers as Corbin Redhounds.

For four decades the 30's, 40's, 50's, and 60's, Corbin High School sports were the glue that held the town together. For those who worked on the railroad, cut or hauled timber, or chiseled and drug coal from the nearby mines, football and basketball was a diversion from the daily chore of providing for their families. Sports were the common denominator that transcended economic levels of Corbin's citizenryThere are others who were prep All-Americans, college All-Americans, NBA and NFL all-stars. *The Boys from Corbin–America's Greatest Little Sports Town* is not just a story...it's a phenomenon.

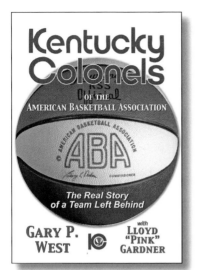

Kentucky Colonels of the American Basketball Association: The Real Story of a Team Left Behind gives an inside look at one of the most intriguing times in the history of professional basketball; and the city of Louisville and the state of Kentucky were enjoying every bit of it.

And then as quickly as the Colonels appeared, they were gone. They had been around just long enough to win a world championship and showcase not only some of the best basketball players in the history of the game, but also some of its most colorful characters.

Perhaps this book should have been written years ago, but there always seemed to be plenty of time. And then one day, a generation or two removed, someone asked what happened to that pro-basketball team back in the 60s and 70s?

BAM, it hits you. This book had to be written.

Here are never-before-told stories that only Lloyd "Pink" Gardner would know. He lived it and Gary P. West wrote it.

A story of colorful owners with family connections to the Lindbergh kidnapping and Hope Diamond; sports agents who would do anything to sign players; a double murder and suicide; a businessman who thought he could do in basketball what he had done with Kentucky Fried Chicken; an insignificant T.V. deal that turned into hundreds of millions of dollars; a team that drafted a 5'6", 55-year-old college professor; and through it all still won a world championship.

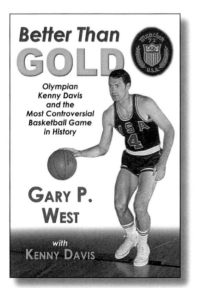

An Olympics like no other…

Every four years in the middle of the summer heat, the whole world turns its eager eyes upon a single gathering of the planet's best athletes for a series of sporting events to determine new thresholds of human excellence, strength, speed and skill, to determine the limit's of the human capacity to perform and to become unequivocally victorious in doing so. In the summer of 1972, however, there occurred such an Olympic gathering much unlike any other before it or, thankfully, since.

Conducted in the aftermath of an unprecedented terrorist attack that had invaded the tranquility of Olympic Village, leaving 11 Israeli athletes dead and the world aghast, was what was to become the most controversial basketball game in the history of the sport. As the USA's team took the court to play for the coveted Gold Medal, a team that had never been defeated in the history of Olympic basketball, there was an unnerving tension building as they prepared to play out the hardwood metaphor for the Cold War itself against the best and most experienced Soviet Union team ever assembled.

This is the story of Kenny Davis, captain of that very team, a sharp-shooting farm boy from Kentucky, cast onto the world's center stage in the challenge of a lifetime. Author Gary West once again rivets the reader to the pages as he relays how the hometown hero Davis' strong rural principles propel him into that position of leadership, poised to take the crushing disappointment that would befall them, and head back home to success as a businessman marketing Converse's famous athletic shoes. Discover what Davis and all of the members of his 1972 USA Olympic Basketball Team did in amidst tragedy and injustice; something much more valuable than just winning a ball game, something much Better Than Gold.